Windows and Apple Macintosh PageM...

Although this book was written specifically for the Wind...
Macintosh users should have little trouble in following the text, since ...
virtually identical on either platform.

If you are a Macintosh user, bear in mind the following:

1.   If a Windows keyboard command makes use of the **Control** key, use
     Command on the Macintosh.

2.   Similarly, replace references to the Windows **Alt** key with **Option**.

3.   Macintosh menus, windows and dialog boxes, whilst containing
     essentially the same information, have a different cosmetic look:

     •   Pop-up menus, indicated by a small downward-pointing arrow in
         Windows, appear as an option within a drop-shadow box on the
         Macintosh.
     •   Macintosh windows have no control menu, in their place is a
         close box (used to shut down the window).
     •   Macintosh file names are not restricted to 8 characters, and can
         use special characters (including spaces). Unlike Windows, the
         type of file is not necessarily indicated as a three-letter suffix.
     •   The Macintosh operating system has its own WIMP filing system
         which does the job of both the Windows File Manager and
         Program Manager.

About the Author

Scott Basham has a BSc. in Computer Science from the University of Edinburgh.
Since then he has spent several years as a computing lecturer.

In 1990 he moved to Aldus UK, where he worked firstly as a Trainer and then as a
Training Consultant responsible for course development. During this time he ran
many training courses for end-users, dealers and staff in the full range of Aldus
software. He has produced PC and Macintosh training material both at Introductory
and Advanced levels. At present he works as a Freelance Training Consultant;
training, lecturing and developing courseware in desktop publishing, including
PageMaker.

Table of Contents

1. The Basics — 9

Introduction — 11
Starting PageMaker — 12
The PageMaker Screen — 13
Floating Palettes — 14
The Rulers — 15
Repositioning the Zero Point — 16
Viewing the Page — 17
Other Page Views — 18

2. Working with a Publication — 19

New Publication — 21
Opening a Publication from Disk — 24
The Page Icons — 25
Inserting/Removing Pages — 26
Saving a Document — 27
Closing a Document — 28

3. The Drawing Tools — 29

Lines — 31
Boxes — 32
Ellipses — 32
Selecting Elements — 33
Deleting Elements — 33
Moving Elements — 34
Resizing Elements — 34
Selecting Multiple Elements — 35
Manipulating Elements using the Control Palette — 37
Moving Elements using the Control Palette — 39
Resizing Elements using the Control Palette — 41
Aligning Elements using the Control Palette — 42
Using Fill and Line — 44
Cut, Copy and Paste — 47
Power Pasting — 48

Multiple Paste _____ 49
Magnetic Guidelines _____ 51
Using Guidelines _____ 53
Defaults _____ 54
The Rotation Tool _____ 57

4. Importing Graphics   59

The Place Command _____ 61
Graphic File Formats _____ 63
Cropping _____ 66
Matching Resolution _____ 67
Image Control _____ 68

5. The Text Tool   69

Adding Text _____ 71
Changing Text _____ 72
Manipulating Text _____ 73
Default Text Settings _____ 75
Working with Blocks of Text _____ 76
More Advanced Text Effects _____ 78

6. Transformations   83

Skewing _____ 85
Reflecting _____ 85
Cropping with the Control Palette _____ 86
Combining Effects _____ 87
Rotating _____ 88

7. Importing Text   89

Placing Text _____ 91
Threaded Text _____ 92
Manipulating Threaded Text Blocks _____ 94
Autoflow _____ 96

8. Master Pages   97

Master Pages _____ 99

Column Guides _____ 100

9. Working with Large Amounts of Text   103

Type Specifications _____ 105
Paragraph Specifications _____ 106
Widows and Orphans _____ 107
The Keep With Command _____ 109
Column and Page Breaks _____ 110
Paragraph Rules _____ 111
Indents/Tabs _____ 113
Hyphenation _____ 116
Inline Graphics _____ 117
Text Wrap _____ 119

10. The Story Editor   121

The Story Editor _____ 123
Features of the Story Editor _____ 124
Story and Layout Views _____ 127

11. Style Sheets   129

Paragraph Styles _____ 131
Using Styles _____ 132
Changing a Style _____ 133
Style by Example _____ 134
Copying Styles from another Document _____ 136

12. Colour   137

The Colour Palette _____ 139
Creating New Colours _____ 139
Importing Colours _____ 142
Colour Libraries _____ 142

13. Aldus Additions   143

Additions _____ 145
Sort Pages _____ 146
Traverse Textblocks _____ 146

Continuation Line _____ 147
Balance Columns _____ 147
Build Booklet _____ 148
Create Colour Library _____ 150
Create Keyline _____ 151
Pub Info _____ 151
Story/Textblock Info _____ 152
Drop Cap _____ 152
Edit Tracks _____ 153
Expert Kerning _____ 155
Open Template _____ 155
PS Group-It/Ungroup-It _____ 156
Other Additions _____ 157

14. The Table Editor 159

The Table Editor _____ 161
Entering Text _____ 162
Importing Text _____ 163
Adjusting Table Dimensions _____ 164
Grouping Cells _____ 165
Changing Text Attributes _____ 166
Lines _____ 167
The Borders Command _____ 168
Fills _____ 169
Number Format _____ 169
Saving and Exporting _____ 170
Using a Table in PageMaker _____ 171
Launching Table Editor from PageMaker _____ 172

15. Links Management 173

The Links Dialog Box _____ 175
Link Status _____ 177
Object Linking using Windows _____ 178

16. Long Document Features 179

The Book Command _____ 181
Table of Contents (TOC) _____ 182

Rebuilding the TOC _____ 184
Indexing _____ 185
Creating the Index _____ 189

17. Printing   191

The Print Document Dialog Box _____ 193
The Print Options Dialog Box _____ 194
The Print Colours Dialog Box _____ 194
The Print Setup Dialog Box _____ 195
Printer Styles _____ 195

18. Tips and Techniques   197

Interruptible Screen Redraw _____ 199
The Magnify Tool _____ 199
The Library Palette _____ 200
Template Documents _____ 202
Creating your own Templates _____ 205
Copying from One Document to Another _____ 206
Using an Outside Printing Service _____ 208
Panose Font Matching _____ 210
Accessing Documents created in an earlier
version of PageMaker _____ 212
Cross Platform Compatibility _____ 212
Compressing TIFF files _____ 214
The Time Stamp Import Filter _____ 216
Special Keyboard Characters _____ 217
Keyboard Shortcut Summary _____ 218
Tips for Good Document Design _____ 220

Index   221

CHAPTER

1

The
Basics

This chapter covers...

Introduction

Starting PageMaker

The PageMaker Screen

Floating Palettes

The Rulers

Repositioning the Zero
Point

Viewing the Page

Other Page Views

Introduction

Desktop Publishing (DTP) can mean different things to different people. Back in 1984, the term DTP was first used to describe the newly released PageMaker version 1. In those days it meant the ability to combine text and graphics on the same page using a personal computer system.

Today many wordprocessors have this capability, while DTP has developed and expanded to cover a much greater range of features and accuracy of control. Systems based on PCs are now being used to create virtually any kind of document previously associated with traditional publishing: from novels and technical manuals to glossy magazines and one-page marketing flyers.

PageMaker version 5 has a rich array of facilities to import text and artwork from other computer application packages, as well as allowing you to generate these directly from within PageMaker itself. It allows precision alignment, sizing and orientation of elements either by using the mouse or by working numerically with dialog boxes and an on-screen control palette. There is a high level of typographical control, as well as a host of features to help with the organisation and management of long documents.

In this guide you will be taken through all the essential features of PageMaker version 5 for Windows. To get the most out of this book, it is recommended that you are first familiar with the Windows operating environment (i.e. using a mouse, icons, menus, dialog boxes etc.). Look at the *Windows in Easy Steps* title in this same series of books for a more complete training and reference on Windows itself.

The objective of this book is to show you PageMaker using pictures and concise explanations rather than endless pages of technical detail. Remember that it is also important to experiment using your own examples; like many things you will find that practice is the key to competence.

Starting PageMaker

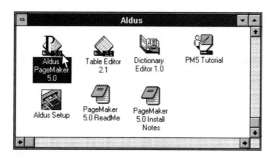

From the Program Manager, you can start PageMaker by double clicking directly on its icon.

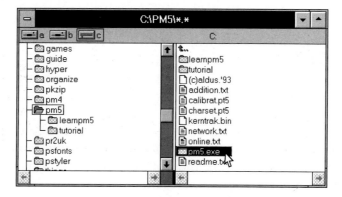

Alternatively, from the File Manager locate the PM5.EXE file and double click.

TIP

Typing "WIN PM5" at the DOS Command prompt will launch Windows and then PageMaker.

NOTE

If you double click on a PM5 file, then your machine will load PageMaker and then automatically open the file:

The PageMaker Screen

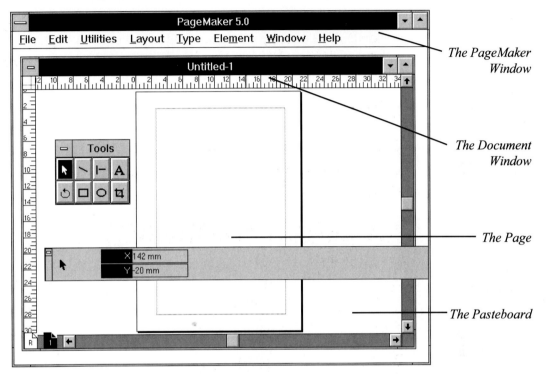

The PageMaker Window

The Document Window

The Page

The Pasteboard

1. Choose **New...** from the File menu. Click **OK**.

The PageMaker screen in arranged as follows:

The PageMaker Window

Double clicking on the control menu will close PageMaker.

The Document Window

You can work on more than one document at a time using PageMaker 5, each with its own window. Note the maximise and minimise buttons will expand the window or shrink it to a single icon.

The Page and Pasteboard

All items positioned on the page will normally be printed. The surrounding pasteboard is a working area.

Floating Palettes

These give you immediate on-screen access to tools and commands. You can move palettes to the most convenient screen position, or close them down altogether if not required.

Double click on the control menu icon to close the palette.

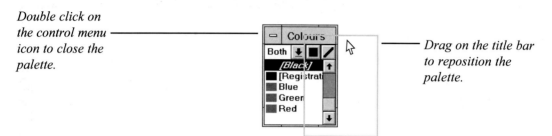

Drag on the title bar to reposition the palette.

Palettes can be turned on and off from the Window menu...

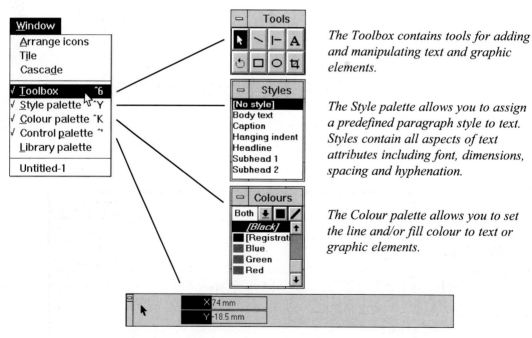

The Toolbox contains tools for adding and manipulating text and graphic elements.

The Style palette allows you to assign a predefined paragraph style to text. Styles contain all aspects of text attributes including font, dimensions, spacing and hyphenation.

The Colour palette allows you to set the line and/or fill colour to text or graphic elements.

The Control palette gives you full numeric control over elements as an alternative to making adjustments manually with the mouse or by dialog box. The controls which appear in the palette depend on the type of element(s) being edited.

The Rulers

The rulers help you make measurements on screen. Dotted line markers appear in each ruler to indicate your current position.

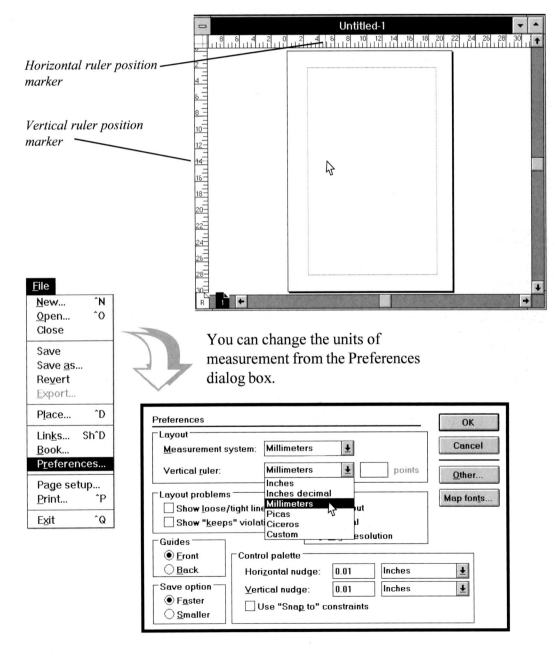

Horizontal ruler position marker

Vertical ruler position marker

You can change the units of measurement from the Preferences dialog box.

Repositioning the Zero Point

Initially all measurements are from the top left corner of the page. This can be changed by moving the Zero point.

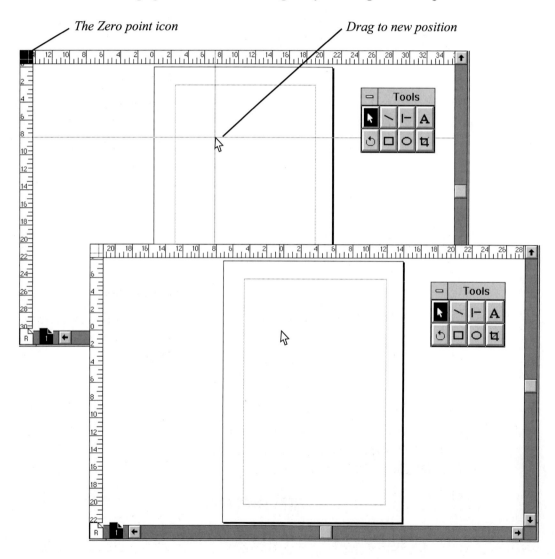

1.   Move the mouse pointer directly over the Zero point icon.

2.   Drag downwards and to the right until you reach the desired position for the new Zero point.

Viewing the Page

There are eight levels of page magnification. The three most often used can be accessed directly with the mouse.

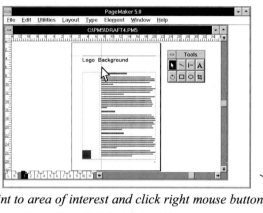

Fit in Window

The page is reduced to a size where it will fit completely in the document window.

Point to area of interest and click right mouse button

Actual Size

The page is displayed the same size as it would be printed.

Click right mouse button while pressing Shift

200% size

The page appears twice the printed size.

Other Page Views

1.   Open the Layout menu.

2.   Select the View submenu.

3.   Choose one of the eight view options. Note that the rulers expand to reveal more detail as you zoom in.

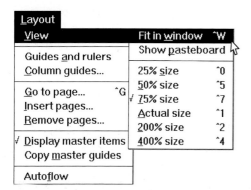

The keyboard shortcuts are listed next to each menu option. The ^ symbol means "hold down the Control key". For example, holding down the Control key while pressing "4" will switch the view to 400% size.

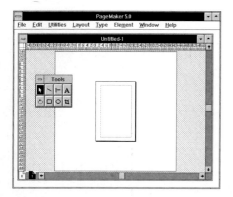

Show Pasteboard

This zooms out to reveal the entire pasteboard area. The shaded area beyond its perimeter is out of bounds.

NOTE

In all views you have access to all PageMaker's layout editing features.

CHAPTER

2

Working with
a Publication

This chapter covers...

New Publication

Opening a Publication
from Disk

The Page Icons

Inserting/Removing
Pages

Saving a Document

Closing a Document

New Publication

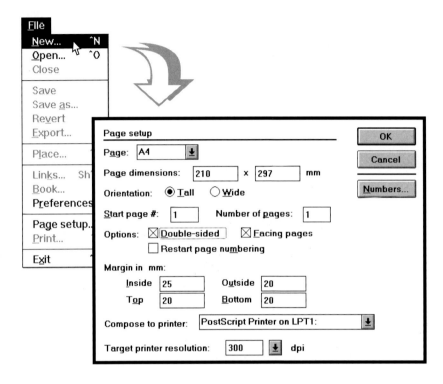

1.   Choose **New...** from the File menu to display the initial Page setup dialog box.

2.   Choose from one of the preset page sizes in the Page pop-up menu, or enter values directly into the Page dimensions boxes (this allows you create a custom page size).

3.   Click on the Tall or Wide radio button to choose Page orientation (note this affects the entire document).

Tall   Wide

4.   The starting page number will normally be 1, but you may change this by entering a value in the Start page # box.

5.   If you know how many pages you require, then enter this value in the Number of pages box. However it is easy to add or remove pages later on.

NOTE

You can view your pages as thumbnail images using the Sort pages Addition (see chapter 13 "Aldus Additions").

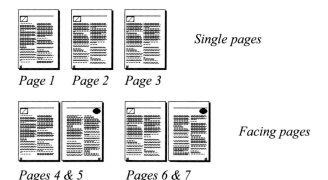

Single pages

Page 1   Page 2   Page 3

Facing pages

Pages 4 & 5   Pages 6 & 7

6. If your document is to be single-sided (printed on only one side of the paper) then remove the cross from the Double-sided checkbox. If the Double-sided option is active then you have a further choice to Display facing pages. This causes PageMaker to show you pages as "spreads" with left and right pages next to each other.

7. If your document is part of a larger Book list (see chapter 16), then you have the option to restart page numbering from this point.

8. Enter your page margins. Note that if your document is double sided then you can set inner and outer margins (the inner margin is at the spine of a bound publication).

9. Choose your target printer from the Compose to printer pop-up menu. This will give you a list of printers installed in Windows. It is important to specify from the outset the printer used for your final, not draft, output if these are different. This gives PageMaker information about the text capabilities, graphics and printable page area which can be used.

10. The output resolution will normally be set automatically according to your choice of printer, but you can alter this manually.

Page numbering

Style: ● Arabic numeral   1, 2, 3, ...
        ○ Upper Roman   I, II, III, ...
        ○ Lower Roman   i, ii, iii, ...
        ○ Upper alphabetic   A, B, C, ... AA, BB, CC, ...
        ○ Lower alphabetic   a, b, c, ... aa, bb, cc, ...

TOC and index prefix: [   ]

OK
Cancel

NOTE

For more information about TOC and index prefix, see chapter 16 "Long Document Features".

11. Click on the Numbers option to alter the style of page numbering. Options include Roman numerals and alphabetic numbering.

File
New...   ^N
Open...   ^O
Close

Save   ^S
Save as...
Revert
Export...

Place...   ^D

Links...   Sh^D
Book...
Preferences...

Page setup...
Print...   ^P

Exit   ^Q

NOTE

*You can return to the Page setup dialog box by choosing **Page setup** from the File menu. In this way you can alter settings even once you have begun work on a document.*

Opening a Publication from Disk

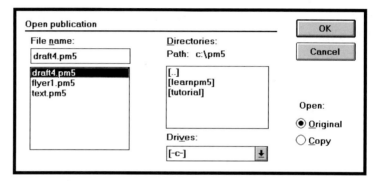

1. Go to the File menu and choose **Open**.

2. The dialog box displays all valid PageMaker files in the current directory. If necessary change directory by typing its path in the File name box or clicking on items in the Directories box.

3. Type or select the filename of the document you wish to open. Click **OK**.

TIP

You can open an untitled copy of an existing document by clicking on the Copy button.

NOTE

In PageMaker 5 you can open as many publications as memory will allow. Each can be activated either by clicking on a visible part of its window or via the Window menu.

The Page Icons

The page icons appear at the bottom left corner of the document window. The currently active page is highlighted.

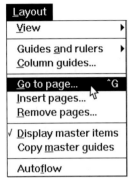

To move to another page simply click on its icon, or use the **Goto page** option from the Layout menu.

TIP

Every time you move to a new page, PageMaker performs a mini-save as a security measure. If your machine crashed during use, you should be able to recover your document. If your document is currently untitled, the mini-saved version will be on disk as a .TMP file.

Master Pages

These appear automatically when a new PageMaker document is created. They are labelled **L** and **R** (**R** only if the document is single sided).

Master pages do not print but they can act as a background for the "real" pages in your publication (see chapter 8).

Inserting/Removing Pages

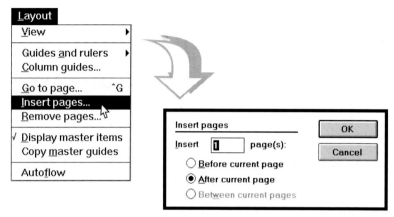

Inserting

1.   Select the page either immediately before or after the place you want the new page(s) to go.

2.   Choose **Insert pages** from the Layout menu.

3.   Enter the number of pages to be inserted.

4.   Select the position for the new pages, either before or after the current page.

NOTE

If you are using a double-sided document, there may be two current pages, and then you can select a third option to add new pages between them.

Removing

The Remove pages... option from the Layout menu works in the same way as Insert pages...

There is an additional warning dialog box which asks you to verify the deletion:

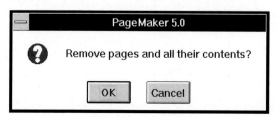

Saving a Document

TIP

If a document has an untitled window then it has not yet been saved.

File

New...	^N
Open...	^O
Close	

Save	
Save as...	
Revert	
Export...	

| Place... | ^D |

Links...	Sh^D
Book...	
Preferences...	

| Page setup... | |
| Print... | ^P |

| Exit | ^Q |

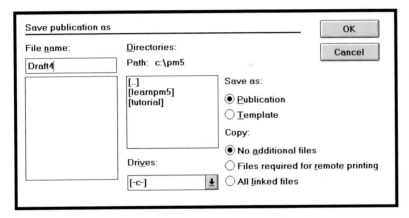

Save publication as   OK

File name: Directories: Cancel

Draft4   Path: c:\pm5

    [..]   Save as:
    [learnpm5]
    [tutorial]   ● Publication
                     ○ Template

                     Copy:

Drives: ● No additional files

[-c-]   ○ Files required for remote printing

                     ○ All linked files

1. If you have more than one publication open, then make active the one you want to save by clicking in its window (or selecting from the Window menu).

2. Choose **Save** from the File menu. If your document already has a name then the save action will be automatic.

3. If you are saving the document for the first time the Save publication as... dialog box will appear. Make sure the correct directory is active (if necessary type in the path or navigate using the Directories box).

4. Type in a valid document name (8 characters or less, no punctuation).

If you wish to save to a file name different to the current document, choose **Save as** from the File menu.

NOTE

You cannot delete or rename files from within PageMaker (you will need to use DOS or the File Manager).

Closing a Document

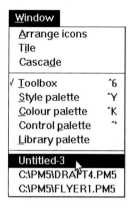

A document is closed when it is no longer required on screen.

1.   If you have more than one document open, then make sure the one you want to close is active. This can be done by clicking on a visible part of the document window, or selecting the document name from the Window menu.

Control box

2.   Either double click on the document's control box or choose **Close** from the File menu.

3.   If the document has not been saved then the following dialog box will appear as a security measure:

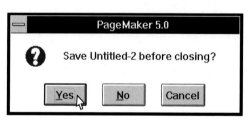

If you click No then the document will close without saving.

Clicking Yes will save your work (you may be asked for a filename if the document is untitled).

Cancel will abort the Close operation and return you to your document window.

CHAPTER

3

The Drawing Tools

This chapter covers...

Lines, Boxes, Ellipses

Selecting Elements

Deleting Elements

Moving Elements

Resizing Elements

Selecting Multiple
Elements

Manipulating Elements

Moving Elements

Resizing Elements

Aligning Elements

Using Fill and Line

Cut, Copy and Paste

Power Pasting

Multiple Paste

Magnetic
Guidelines

Using Guidelines

Defaults

The Rotation Tool

Lines

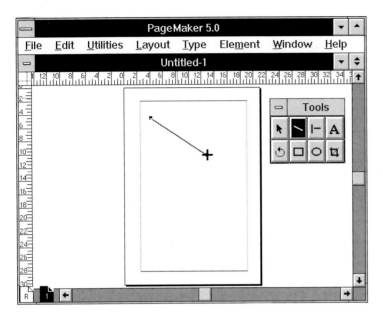

1. Select the Line tool from the toolbox. Your pointer will turn into a cross (to aid accurate drawing).

2. Drag from one end of the line to another.

The Line Tool

The Perpendicular Line Tool

This will draw lines at 45 degree intervals, i.e. horizontally, vertically or diagonally.

HINT

*You can achieve the same effect with the normal line tool if you hold down the **Shift** key while drawing.*

The Perpendicular Line Tool

Boxes

The Box Tool

To draw a rectangle, select the box tool and drag from one corner to the other.

Ellipses

The Ellipse Tool

To draw an oval shape, select the ellipse tool and drag diagonally.

HINT

If you hold down Shift when drawing, all shapes will be made regular.

Boxes will be kept square, and ellipses constrained as circles.

Selecting Elements

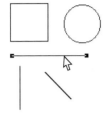

Normally, the element most recently drawn is selected.

You can tell that a shape is selected by the square handles (blocks) which appear at each end.

To select an element

1.   Choose the pointer tool.

2.   Click directly on the shape with the tip of the pointer.

The Pointer Tool

Deleting Elements

1.   Select the element to be deleted

2.   Press the Delete key.

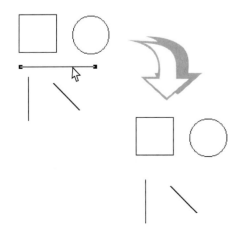

Moving Elements

1. Select the element to be moved.

2. Drag to the new location.

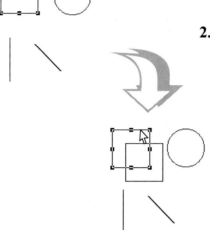

Resizing Elements

1. Select the element to be resized.

2. Drag directly on one of its handles.

NOTE

Dragging on an edge handle will let you resize a shape horizontally or vertically, whilst dragging on a corner handle lets you stretch in both directions at once.

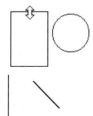
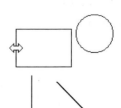
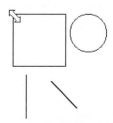

Selecting Multiple Elements

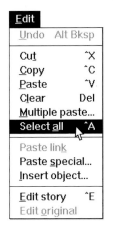

To select all elements on the page and pasteboard choose **Select all** from the Edit menu.

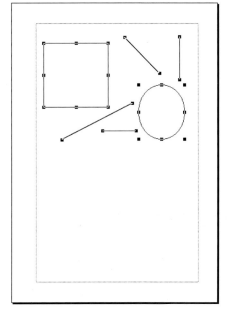

Shift-Clicking

Normally when you click on an object any previously selected objects will be deselected.

If you hold down **Shift**, you can click on as many objects as you wish.

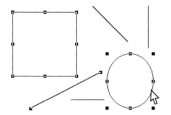

TIP

Shift-clicking on an already-selected object will deselect it. This allows you to switch objects on and off at will.

Creating a Selection Box

1.   Select the pointer tool

2.   Move to a blank area of page or pasteboard.

3.   Drag diagonally. As you drag a box bordered by a dotted line will appear.

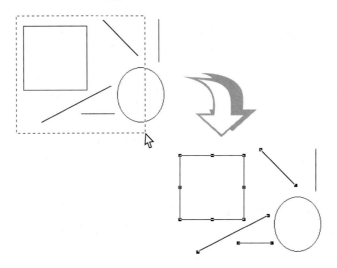

4.   When you release the mouse button, all objects *completely* enclosed by this box will be selected.

Summary

Three ways to make multiple selections:

•   Select all

•   Shift clicking

•   Selection box

TIP

You could use a combination of these techniques, e.g. Select all followed by Shift-Click on one element (to deselect) will have the overall effect of selecting all but one element on the page/ pasteboard.

Manipulating Elements using the Control Palette

NOTE

If the Control palette is not active: choose the Control Palette option from the Window menu.

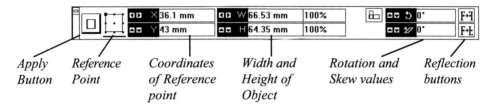

Apply Button   *Reference Point*   *Coordinates of Reference point*   *Width and Height of Object*   *Rotation and Skew values*   *Reflection buttons*

In PageMaker 5 you have the choice to manipulate elements either visually using the mouse, or numerically with the Control palette.

The Control palette gives you the opportunity to specify the size, position or special effects on an object with complete precision.

Resizing

1. Select the element to be resized. The Control palette will display the object's attributes.

2. Edit the width and height values within the Control palette.

3. Click on the Apply button.

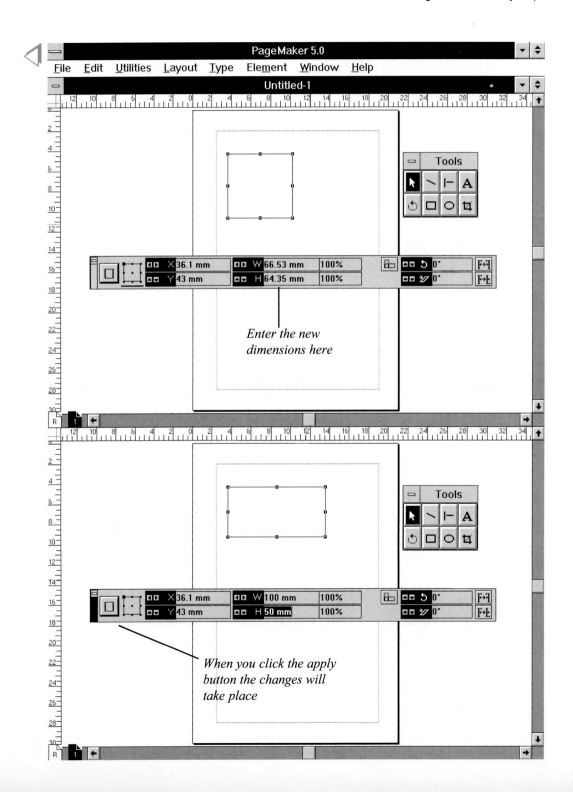

Enter the new
dimensions here

When you click the apply
button the changes will
take place

Moving Elements using the Control Palette

When moving an element using the control palette, you can set the reference point by clicking on the symbol at the left of the control palette.

Changing the Coordinates of the Top Left Corner of a Shape

1. Select the shape with the Pointer tool.

2. Make sure the top left reference point is active by clicking on its symbol in the Control palette. The point should be marked by a small square block (if it is marked by a double arrow then click once more on the point).

3. Type in the new coordinates for this point.

Click here to select the top left reference point (repositioning mode).

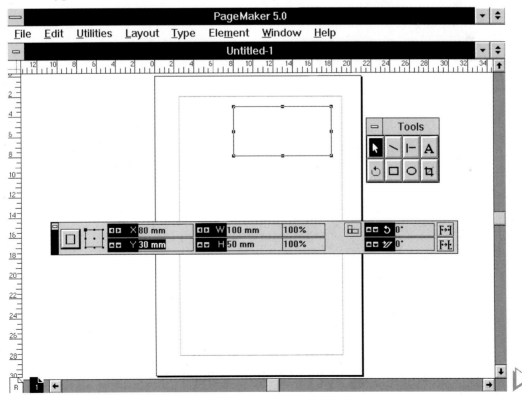

4.   Click on the Apply button. The shape will be moved so
      that its top left corner has the specified coordinates.

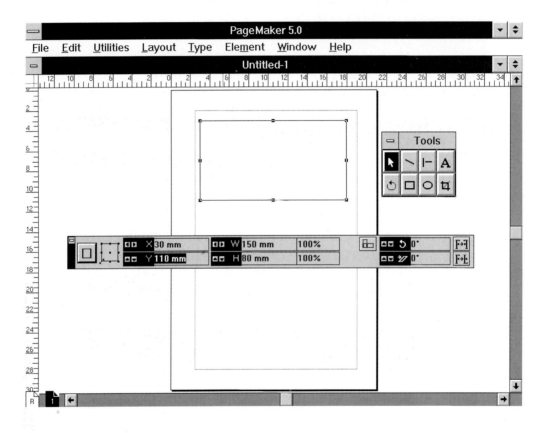

Resizing Elements using the Control Palette

1. Select the shape to be resized.

2. Choose the reference point by clicking on the Control palette symbol. If necessary, click a second time to ensure that the point is marked by a double arrow (this arrow indicates that resizing mode is active).

Lower left reference point selected (resizing mode).

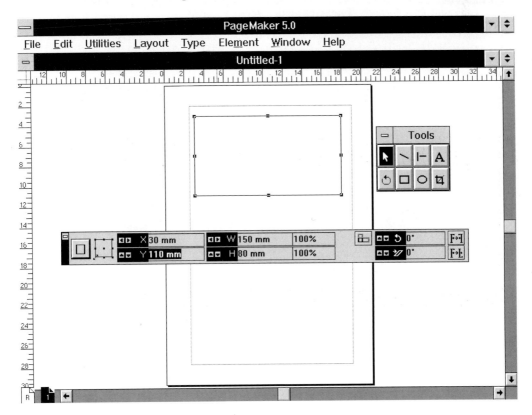

3. Enter the new coordinates for this point.

4. Click on the Apply button. The shape will be resized so that the required point has the given coordinates.

Aligning Elements using the Control Palette

In this example we have two elements we wish to align. We would like to move the circle so that its centre is directly below that of the rectangle...

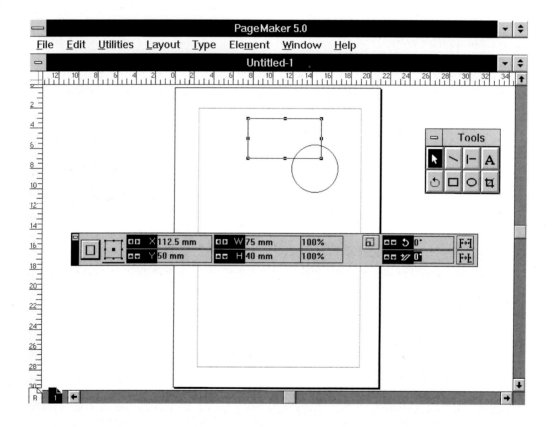

1. Click on the first shape (the rectangle) with the pointer tool and make the centre reference point active.

2. Note the X coordinate, in this case 112.5mm.

3. Click on the second shape (the circle).

4. Enter the same X value, 112.5mm.

5. Click on the apply button. The circle's centre will now have the same X coordinate value as that of the rectangle.

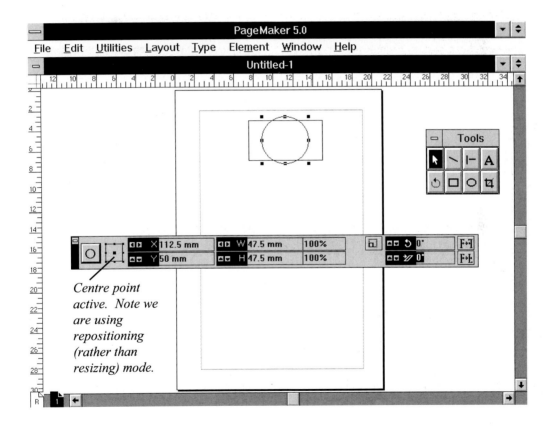

Centre point active. Note we are using repositioning (rather than resizing) mode.

Using Fill and Line

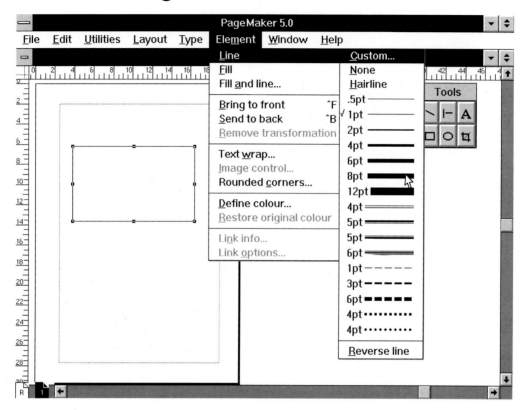

Changing Line Style

1. Select the element(s) to be changed.

2. Choose **Line** from the Element menu.

3. Select the desired line style.

Changing an Element's Fill

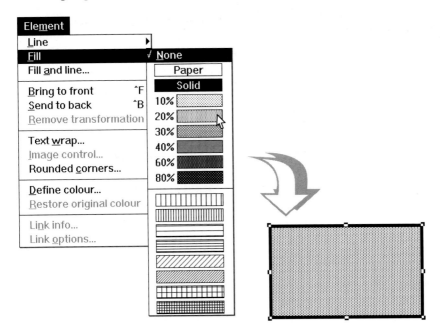

1. Select the element(s) to be changed.

2. Choose **Fill** from the Element menu.

3. Select the desired fill.

TIP

You can control the line style more accurately by using the Custom line option from the Element menu.

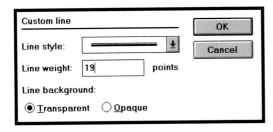

Here you can specify an exact line weight as well as style type.

TIP

The Fill and line dialog box (Element menu) allows you to specify both colour and type of fill and line in one operation.

Fill and line				OK
Fill:	20% 0 ⬇	Line:	Custom... ⬇	Cancel
Color:	Black ⬇	Color:	Black ⬇	
☐ Overprint		☐ Overprint		

HINT

Note the subtle difference between a shape filled with "none", and another filled with "paper". The paper-filled shape is opaque - objects behind it cannot be seen.

The unfilled shape can only be selected from its perimeter, whereas a shape with any type of fill can be moved or selected from any point on its surface.

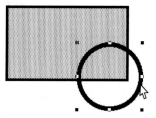

Select/move from edge only

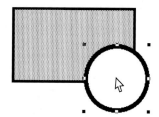

Select/move from any part of the object

Cut, Copy and Paste

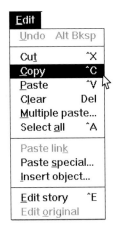

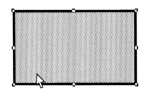

Copying

1. Select the Element(s).

2. Choose **Copy** from the Edit menu. A copy of the element(s) will be made and stored in the Clipboard.

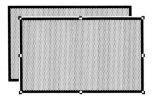

3. Choose **Paste** from the Edit menu. The Clipboard contents will be copied back to the page, slightly offset from the original.

4. Position the new element(s) as desired.

TIP

*Choosing **Paste** does not deplete the Clipboard contents, so pasting several times will give you additional copies.*

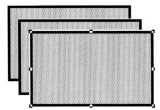

Cut

1. Select one or more elements.

2. Choose **Cut** from the Edit menu. The shapes will disappear from the page or pasteboard and are moved into the Clipboard.

3. To bring back the elements, choose **Paste**. This is useful when you want to move shapes from one page to another. For example, you may cut all elements from page 3, turn to page 7, and then paste them back.

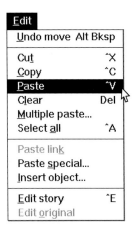

Power Pasting

1.   Select an element with the pointer tool.

2.   Choose **Copy** from the Edit menu.

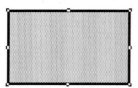

3.   Instead of **Paste**, type **Control-Shift-P**. The copy will
      appear positioned directly over the original. (This is useful
      if you want to copy items from one page to another whilst
      maintaining their exact position).

4.   Move the new element by dragging with the pointer tool.
      Make sure that you move it only once, and do not deselect.

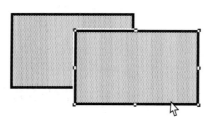

NOTE

*Instead of manually dragging
the shape, you could adjust its
position numerically with the
control palette.*

5.   Type **Control-Shift-P** again. An additional copy will
      appear offset by the same distance as exists between the
      first two elements.

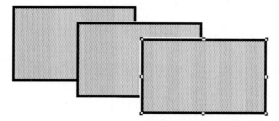

6.   You can use **Control-Shift-P** to produce more copies at
      equal intervals. This technique is known as Power Pasting.

Multiple Paste

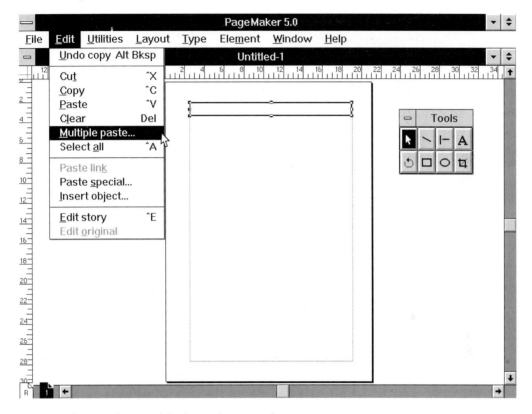

1. Select a shape with the pointer tool.

2. Choose **Copy** from the Edit menu.

3. Choose **Multiple paste** also from the Edit menu.

4. In the dialog box which appears, enter the number of copies required and the offsets (vertical and horizontal) for each successive copy.

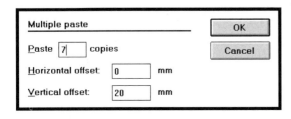

In this example seven copies
are made, each 20mm
directly below its neighbour.

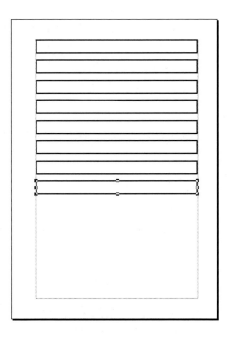

Magnetic Guidelines

Provided the **Snap-to** option is active (from the Layout menu, Guides and rulers submenu), you will notice that the page margins are magnetic, i.e. elements tend to "snap-to" the margin lines once within a certain distance. This makes it easy to align elements.

Setting your own Vertical Guide Lines

1.   With the pointer tool, move into the vertical ruler (the arrow should turn white).

2.   Drag onto the page. The arrow will become double-headed and a light blue vertical guideline will appear in-between.

3.   You can reposition this guide at any time, or delete by dragging it back onto the pasteboard.

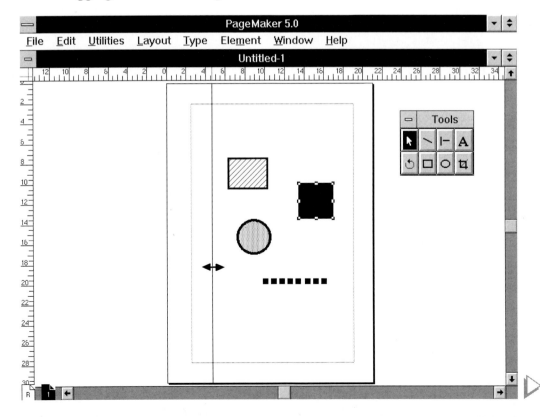

Creating Horizontal Guidelines

These are created in the same way:

1.   Move into the horizontal ruler, and drag down onto the page.

2.   You can repeat this process to create more guidelines, as long as the total count of horizontal plus vertical does not exceed 40.

HINT

*Guides normally appear in front of PageMaker elements. Sometimes this may make it difficult to see thin objects such as hairlines. There is, however, an option to display guides "at the back" in the **Preferences** dialog box (File menu).*

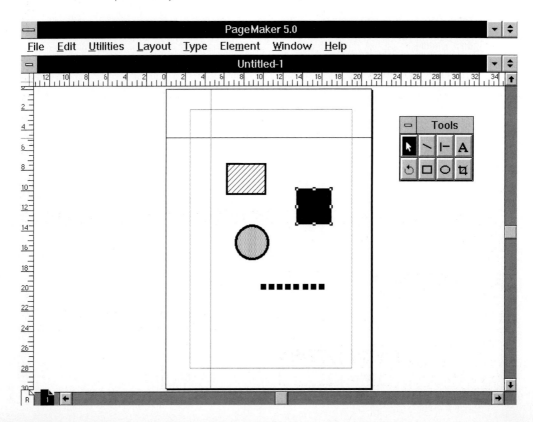

Using Guidelines

Provided the "snap to" feature is active (Layout menu, Guides and rulers submenu), all guidelines will be magnetic. As you move or resize shapes using the mouse, they will snap into place when close to a guideline. This helps you to control the structure of your page design.

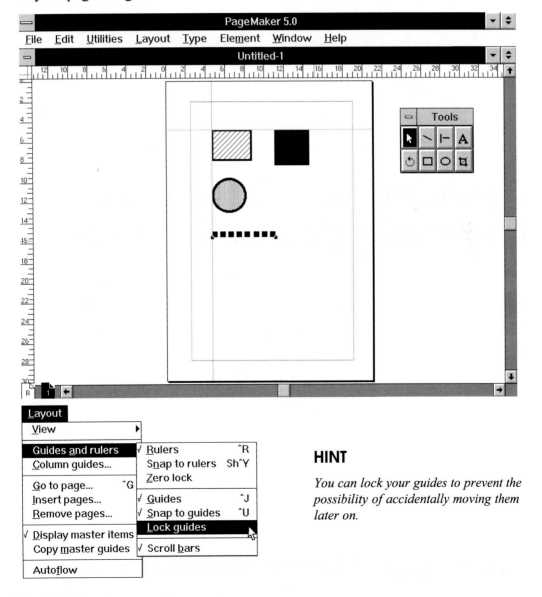

HINT

You can lock your guides to prevent the possibility of accidentally moving them later on.

Defaults

Defaults determine the initial effects applied to newly created PageMaker elements.

For example, if the defaults have not been changed since PageMaker was installed, you will find that all new shapes have a default line style of one point, and a default fill of none.

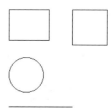

Changing a document's default line style

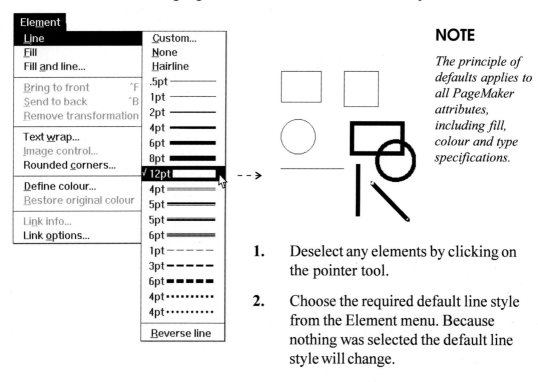

NOTE

The principle of defaults applies to all PageMaker attributes, including fill, colour and type specifications.

1. Deselect any elements by clicking on the pointer tool.

2. Choose the required default line style from the Element menu. Because nothing was selected the default line style will change.

3. In the above example all new shapes will now initially have a line style of 12 points.

Changing PageMaker's global defaults

The previous example demonstrated altering defaults which apply to the working document only. This information is always saved as part of the document file.

It is also possible to change the global defaults, which will affect initial default values for all new PageMaker documents.

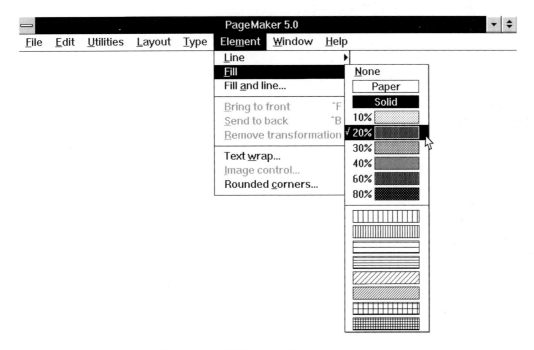

1.   Close any open documents (File menu).

2.   Any settings you make now will change PageMaker's general defaults. In this example from now onwards all new PageMaker documents will use a 20% grey fill for boxes and circles.

TIP

*Choosing **Page setup** from the File menu at this time will let you specify default attributes for new documents.*

The PM5.CNF file

This file contains PageMaker's global default information. You may wish to access this file (from DOS or the File Manager) for the following reasons:

1.   **Restoring defaults to the factory settings**

Simply delete the PM5.CNF file. A new one will be created the next time you launch PageMaker.

2.   **Backing up default settings**

If you back up PM5.CNF to a floppy disk, you will be able to restore your default settings later on by copying the file back again. This is particularly useful if someone else has been using your machine and changing the settings from those which you prefer.

3.   **Copy defaults to other machines**

Simply copy the PM5.CNF file to the same directory on other machines which have PageMaker 5 installed. This allows you to develop company-wide standards for text and graphic defaults (including colour schemes and corporate fonts) on one PC which you may then copy across to others.

The Rotation Tool

This allows you to freely rotate any PageMaker element directly on screen using the mouse

The rotation tool

1. Select the item to be rotated.

2. Choose the Rotation tool.

3. Move to the point where you wish the *pivot* for rotation to be. Hold down the mouse button and drag several centimetres to the right. (Do not let go of the button yet.)

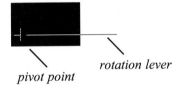

pivot point   *rotation lever*

TIP

The further you initially drag from the pivot point, the better your control over the rotation angle.

4. A line will appear which can be used as a rotation lever. By dragging in a circular motion around the pivot point you can rotate the element in either a clockwise or anticlockwise direction.

dragging in a clockwise direction about the pivot point

5. When you have achieved the desired angle, release the mouse button. The element has been rotated.

TIP

If the control palette is active, then you will be able to read off the angle of rotation in degrees as you rotate.

NOTE

To rotate using the numeric control palette, see chapter 6 "Transformations".

CHAPTER

4

Importing
Graphics

This chapter covers...

The Place Command

Graphic File Formats

Cropping

Matching Resolution

Image Control

The Place Command

Graphics generated in other applications packages can be brought into a PageMaker document by using the **Place** command.

1. Choose **Place** from the File menu. The Place dialog box will appear.

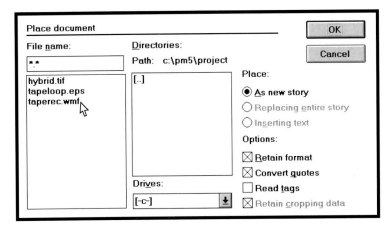

2. Use the directory list to find the location of the file to be imported, or type the path manually.

3. Either type the filename followed by **Return** or double click directly on a name displayed in the directory list.

4. Back on the page, your pointer will change into a loaded graphic icon. This gives you the opportunity to decide where the graphic will be positioned initially.

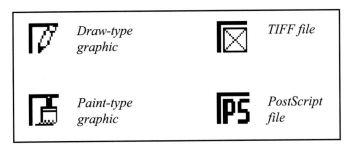

Loaded icons indicating type of graphic file about to be imported.

5.   Position the loaded icon and click once.

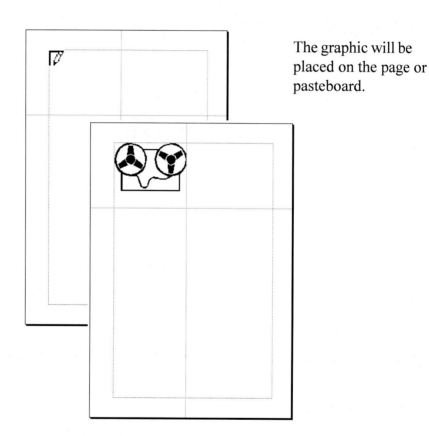

The graphic will be placed on the page or pasteboard.

TIP

PageMaker can read a wide selection of different file formats, text and graphic, depending on the import filters selected at installation time.

*To find out which filters have been installed, hold down the **Control** key and choose **About PageMaker** from the Help menu.*

To install additional filters, double click on the Aldus Setup icon from the Program Manager.

Graphic File Formats

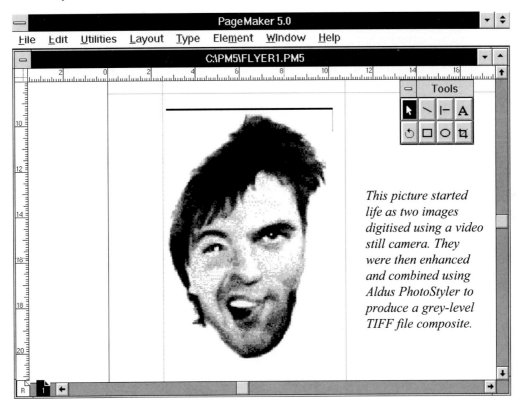

Bitmapped Graphics

TIFF files and Paint files are bitmapped. This means that they are represented as a series of dots (or blocks) which build up an image.

It is important to note the *resolution* of bitmapped graphics. If the resolution is high then the component dots will be small, which improves the quality of the image. Resolution is normally measured in dots per inch (dpi).

NOTE

High resolution images look clearer when printed out (provided the printer can match the resolution), but take up proportionately more storage space.

At 400% view size you can clearly see the blocks which make up the image...

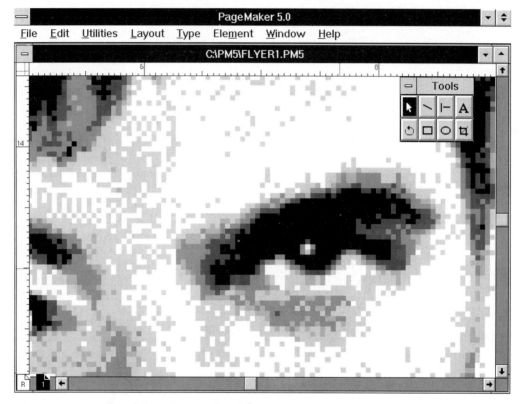

Resizing Imported Graphics

1. Click on the element with the Pointer tool

HINT

Remember that you can also move or resize any element using the Control Palette. This will give you precise numeric control (see chapter 3).

2. Resize in the normal way (as for native PageMaker elements) by dragging on the object handles.

3. Hold down the **Shift** key if you want the graphic to remain in its original proportions.

Moving Imported Graphics

1. Again, select the element with the pointer tool and then move by dragging anywhere within the shape.

Draw-Type Graphics

These are stored not as images, but as objects. The graphic is created as a series of (sometimes complex) mathematical shapes, and redrawn to any required resolution.

The draw-type loaded graphic icon.

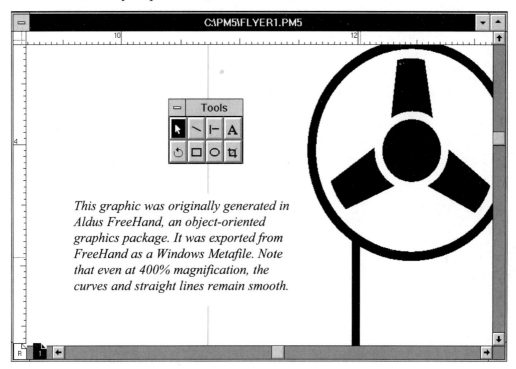

You can freely resize these graphics without losing definition. The final resolution is determined by the output device.

EPS stands for Encapsulated PostScript. This is a page description language, a widely used standard in professional printing. EPS files may contain a combination of bitmapped and draw-type graphics as well as text.

EPS Files

Since PostScript is a printer language, your EPS file may not display on the screen. Some EPS files get around this by incorporating a TIFF preview image, which may still look "grainier" than the final printed version.

Cropping

The Cropping Tool

Cropping is used to "cut away" any unwanted parts of an imported graphic.

1.   Select the Cropping tool from the Toolbox.

2.   Click once on the imported graphic to display its handles.

3.   Line up the *centre* of the cropping tool with a handle.

4.   Hold down the mouse button, you may have to wait a few seconds while the image is prepared for cropping.

5.   Drag towards the centre of the object. Part of the image will disappear.

dragging inwards with the cropping tool

6.   Repeat this process with other handles if necessary.

Dragging within the shape with the cropping tool

HINT

If you move within the shape and then hold down the mouse button, the cropping icon will change into a grabber hand. You will then be able to reposition the whole shape within its cropped "window".

NOTE

Cropping is non-destructive. This means that you can always restore the shape by pulling the handles back out again.

Matching Resolution

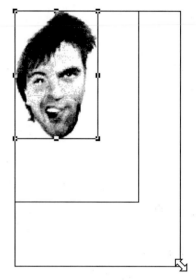

1. Make sure that your final output device has been selected (Page setup from the File menu). This lets PageMaker know which resolutions of bitmapped image will work best when printed.

2. Select any bitmapped graphic (i.e. a paint-type or TIFF file).

3. Resize the image by dragging on a handle, but with the **Control** key depressed. The graphic will resize in "jumps", as PageMaker only allows sizes which will print with maximum clarity on the selected printing device.

NOTE

This does not apply to imported Draw-type or EPS graphics.

Image Control

TIP

Image Control can be used to help "balance" several images on the page, so they appear to have the same lightness and contrast.

1. Select an imported TIFF file with the pointer tool.

2. Choose **Image control** from the Element menu.

3. The following dialog box will appear:

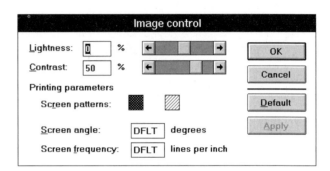

4. Make a change and click the **Apply** button to preview the effect on the image.

5. Click **OK** when satisfied, or **Cancel** to abort.

Lightness increased to 30%

Contrast increased to 100% (pure black and white)

Contrast of minus 50% (inverted image)

NOTE

Screening is the process where grey levels are simulated with solid black dots. This is done by printing a fine pattern of dots; the further apart the dots the lighter the overall grey effect.

This also applies to colour - for example screened red dots will simulate a shade of pink.

CHAPTER

5

The Text
Tool

This chapter covers...

Adding Text

Changing Text

Manipulating Text

Default Text Settings

Working with Blocks
of Text

More Advanced Text
Effects

Adding Text

1. Select the Text tool.

2. Click anywhere on the page within the margin guides. An insertion point (text cursor) will appear at the left margin.

3. Type in the text.

The Text tool

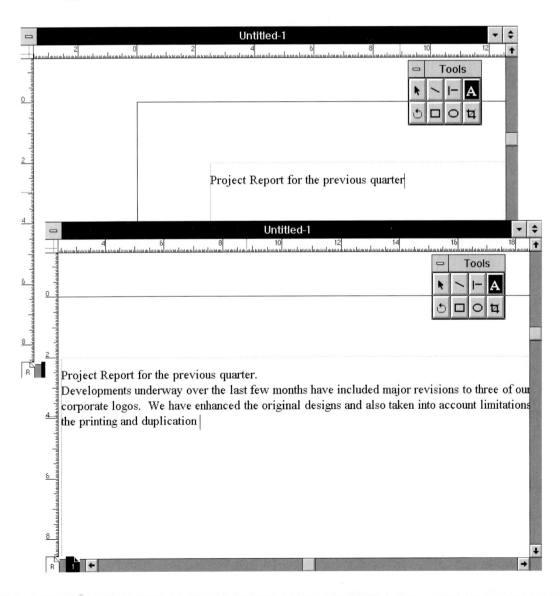

Changing Text

1.   With the Text tool, drag across the text you wish to select.

2.   You now have the opportunity to make changes to this
     text.

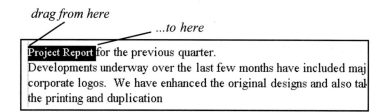

drag from here

...to here

Project Report for the previous quarter.
Developments underway over the last few months have included maj
corporate logos. We have enhanced the original designs and also tal
the printing and duplication

3.   You can use the Control palette to alter any of the text
     attributes. Note that changes only affect the selected text.

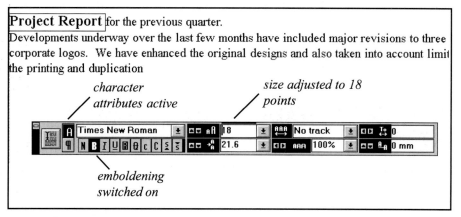

Project Report for the previous quarter.
Developments underway over the last few months have included major revisions to three
corporate logos. We have enhanced the original designs and also taken into account limit
the printing and duplication

*character
attributes active*

*size adjusted to 18
points*

*emboldening
switched on*

Other Ways to Select Text

Double click: Selects a word.

Triple click: Selects the surrounding paragraph.

Select all: (From the Edit menu) Selects all text in
                  a story.

Shift-click: Selects from previous insertion point to
                  mouse location.

Manipulating Text

Selected text can be copied, cut and pasted (from the Edit menu) in the same manner as graphics (see chapter 3).

Changing text attributes is achieved most easily with the Control palette. This operates in two modes: character and paragraph level.

Character Level Attributes

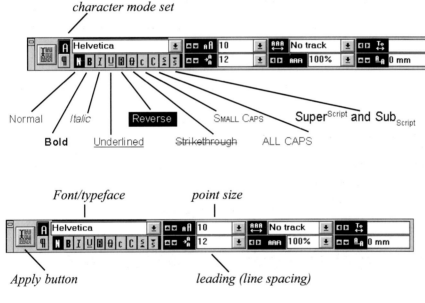

character mode set

Normal   *Italic*   Reverse   SMALL CAPS   Super^{Script} and Sub$_{Script}$

Bold   Underlined   Strikethrough   ALL CAPS

Font/typeface   *point size*

Apply button   *leading (line spacing)*

NOTE

Reverse text is the same colour as the paper, so you will need to create a black box behind if it is to be seen.

TIP

To see how the changes affect the text, click on the Apply button, or press Escape to abort the new setting.

1.   Activate or deactivate an effect (e.g. bold) by clicking once on its icon.

2.   Select a font from the pop-up menu.

3.   Enter a new point size or select from the pop-up menu.

4.   Leading is the vertical space given to a line of text (usually measured in points). An automatic setting is available from the pop-up menu.

▷

Paragraph Level Attributes

These are characteristics which affect entire paragraphs of text.

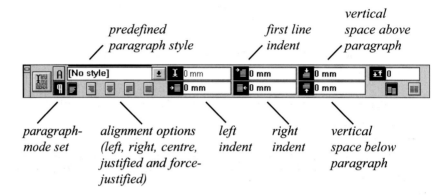

predefined paragraph style *first line indent* *vertical space above paragraph*

paragraph-mode set *alignment options (left, right, centre, justified and force-justified)* *left indent* *right indent* *vertical space below paragraph*

Examples of Paragraph Settings

> This text has a space below paragraph of 5mm. It is left aligned with a first line indent of 10mm.
>
> This paragraph uses centre alignment.

> This text is justified. This means that space is adjusted between words/letters so that each line begins and ends at the same place, apart from this final line.
> **Force justification affects all lines in the paragraph.**

NOTE

For more information about predefined paragraph styles, see chapter 11 "Style Sheets".

Menu Options

Individual settings may also be made using the Type menu. Note that some of these options have keyboard shortcuts listed.

Default Text Settings

Setting Document Defaults

1. Make sure that no text is selected, and no insertion point active. The best way to do this is to click on the Pointer tool.

2. Make the required settings from the Control palette or Type menu.

3. From now on all new text created in the current document will initially have these new attributes.

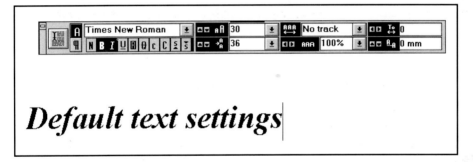

Setting PageMaker Global Text Defaults

1. Close all documents.

2. Make the required text settings. These are automatically saved in the PM5.CNF file (see Chapter 3 - Defaults).

Working with Blocks of Text

If you click on your text with the pointer tool, it will be treated as a single PageMaker element: a text block. This can be moved or resized without altering the attributes of the text within.

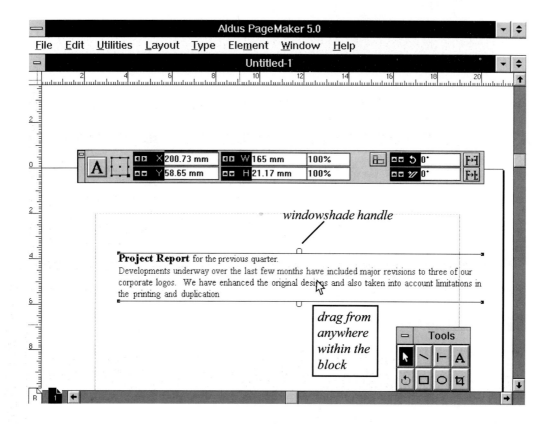

NOTE

You cannot alter the text attributes with the Pointer, only the Text tool.

Moving a Text Block

1. Select with the pointer tool.

2. Drag from anywhere within the block (avoid the handles).

Text blocks have two extra handles known as windowshades. These are normally blank but are sometimes used to indicate text which is continued to or from another block.

Resizing Text Blocks

This can be done either by dragging on the object's handles or via the control palette:

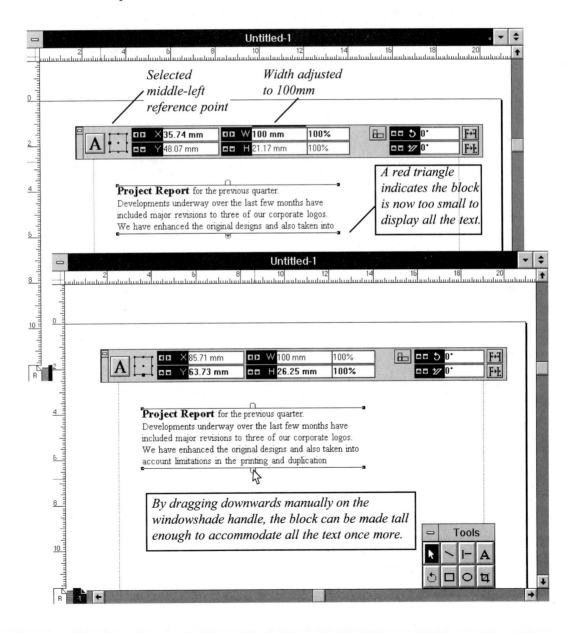

More Advanced Text Effects

Kerning

If all characters are evenly spaced out, some combinations of letters give the illusion of too much horizontal space:

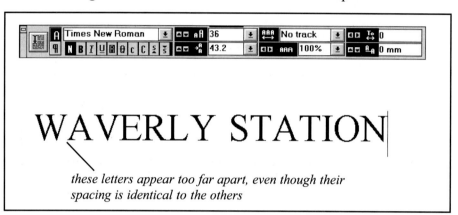

these letters appear too far apart, even though their spacing is identical to the others

PageMaker recognises these pairs of characters automatically, and will adjust accordingly. This is known as automatic pair kerning (accessible from the Type menu; Paragraph; Spacing):

space adjusted automatically

Kerning can also be carried out manually:

1.   Click an insertion point (using the text tool) between the characters to be kerned.

2.   Press **Control** and **Backspace** to kern the characters together. **Control**, **Shift** and **Backspace** will move them further apart.

Also,

1.   You can kern a range of characters by firstly selecting them with the text tool.

2.   You can use the Control palette for full numeric control over kerning, as in the example below:

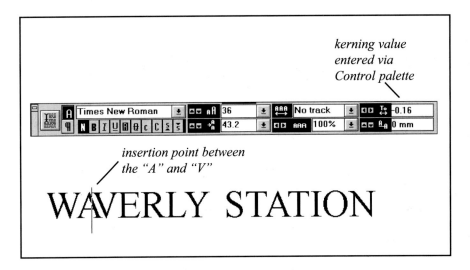

kerning value entered via Control palette

insertion point between the "A" and "V"

Tracking

This is similar to kerning in that it deals with the horizontal space between letters.

Tracking is a paragraph level attribute which takes note of the font and the size of the text to which it applies. PageMaker has five intelligent tracking algorithms, ranging from **Very tight** through **Normal** to **Very loose**.

Tracking can be applied either from the Type menu or the Control palette:

NOTE

In general, tracking keeps big characters closer together - since spacing is much more noticeable at large point sizes.

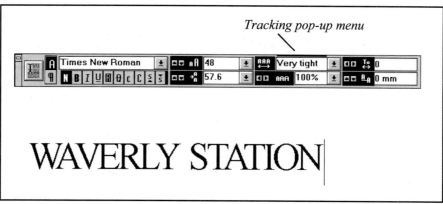

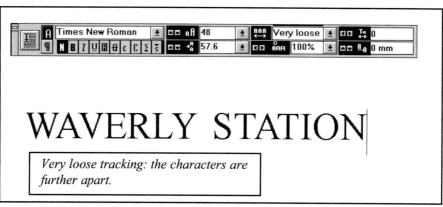

Very loose tracking: the characters are
further apart.

Shift Baseline

1.   Select the required characters with the Text tool.

2.   Enter the baseline shift value into the Control palette. A
     negative value indicates a shift downwards.

3.   Click the Apply button.

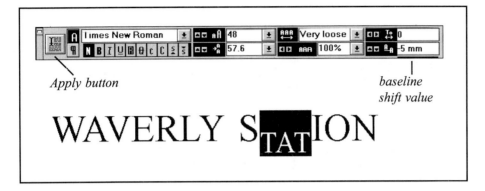

Apply button

baseline shift value

Set Width

This scales text horizontally by a given percentage, without altering its vertical point size. This can be done either from the Type menu or by the Control palette as a character level attribute:

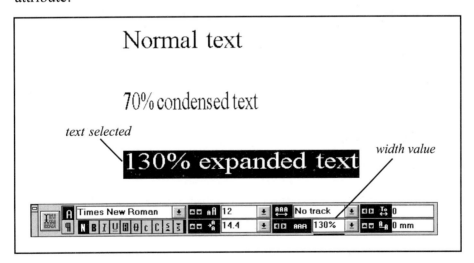

CHAPTER

Transformations

This chapter covers...

Skewing

Reflecting

Cropping with the
Control Palette

Combining Effects

Rotating

Skewing

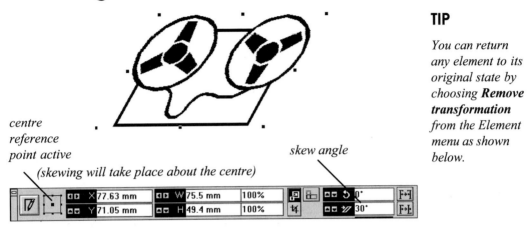

centre
reference
point active

(skewing will take place about the centre)

skew angle

| | | X | 77.63 mm | | | W | 75.5 mm | 100% | | | | | | ↺ | 0° | |→→| |
| | | Y | 71.05 mm | | | H | 49.4 mm | 100% | | | | | | ∥ | 30° | |→↓| |

1. Select the object and reference point.

2. Enter the skew angle and click the Apply button.

Reflecting

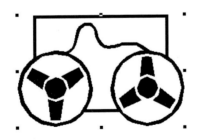

| | | X | 79.04 mm | | | W | 75.5 mm | 100% | | | | | | ↺ | 0° | |→→| |
| | | Y | 71.6 mm | | | H | 49.4 mm | 100% | | | | | | ∥ | 0° | |→↓| |

horizontal
reflection

vertical
reflection

1. Select the object and reference point.

2. Click on either the horizontal or vertical reflection icon.

Cropping with the Control Palette

*middle left
reference point*

*width reduced to half
its initial value*

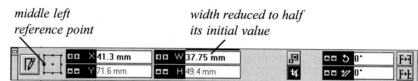

1. Select the element for cropping and choose a reference point. In this example we are using the left middle object handle.

2. You can now either adjust the reference point's coordinates, or edit the overall width/height of the object. The element will be cropped to accommodate the changes. In this case we have adjusted the width to exactly half its previous value.

Combining Effects

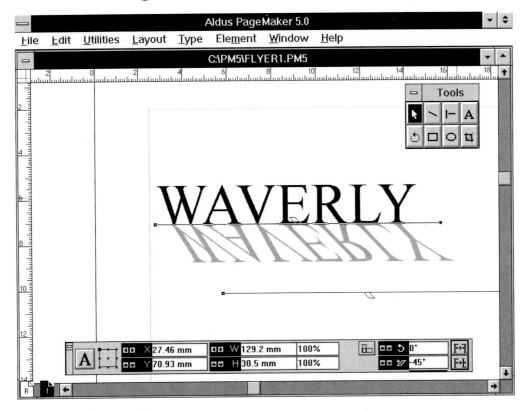

In the above example the following steps were taken:

1. The text block was selected, then **Copy** and **Paste** (from the Edit menu) were chosen.

2. The copy was vertically reflected using the icon in the Control palette.

3. It was then skewed minus 45 degrees about its top left corner.

4. A 30% grey colour was applied (see chapter 12 "Colour").

5. The transformed element was positioned accordingly.

Rotating

Using the Control Palette

1. Make sure the Control palette is active (Window menu).

2. Select the element for rotation.

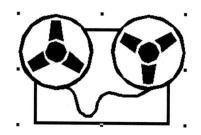

3. Choose the reference point (in this example we shall rotate
    the object about its centre).

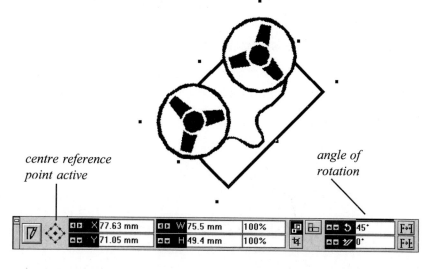

*centre reference
point active*

*angle of
rotation*

4. Enter the angle of rotation and then click the Apply button.

CHAPTER

7

Importing Text

This chapter covers...

Placing Text

Threaded Text

Manipulating Threaded
Text Blocks

Autoflow

Placing Text

This is exactly the same as importing graphics:

1. Choose **Place** from the File menu. The place dialog box will appear.

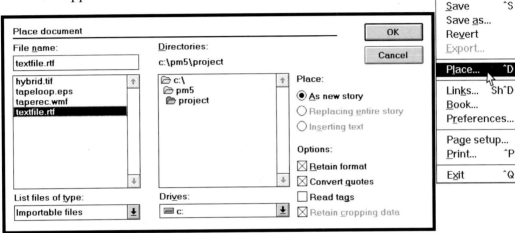

2. Locate the file to be placed by using the directory box or by typing the path in the File name box.

3. Either enter the filename or select the required file from the directory box and click **OK**.

4. PageMaker will return to layout view - your pointer a loaded text icon. Click somewhere inside the page margins (or where you wish the top left corner of the text block to be). The text will flow onto the page.

Text place symbol (loaded icon)

NOTE

When importing text, PageMaker only ever works with its own private copy of the original file. This allows you to freely edit the placed text without disturbing the source document.

The text will normally flow within the page margins.

TIP

If you click and drag with the loaded text icon you can pre-draw the text box into which the story will be placed.

Threaded Text

A small red triangle in the lower windowshade handle indicates that there is more text than can be displayed. To remedy this you can:

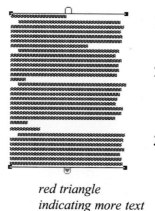

red triangle indicating more text to be placed

1. Increase the block size by dragging on a handle.

2. Decrease the size of the text using the Control palette or Type menu.

3. Create an additional text box (or boxes) into which the story may be continued.

To Thread Text into Another Block

1. Click once directly on the red triangle using the pointer tool. The pointer will turn into the loaded text icon once more, giving you the opportunity to place a second text block.

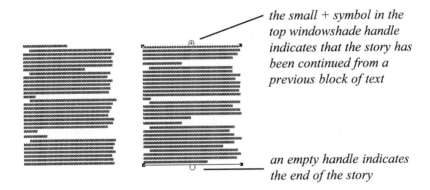

the small + symbol in the top windowshade handle indicates that the story has been continued from a previous block of text

an empty handle indicates the end of the story

2. Click to place the second block. There is still only one story, but it is now threaded through two text blocks.

You can use this technique to thread a story through three or more text blocks. The + symbols in the windowshade handles remind you that the blocks are linked.

Selecting with the Text Tool

1. Click anywhere inside a block with the Text tool.

2. Choose Select all from the Edit menu. The text in all of the threaded blocks will be selected.

Manipulating Threaded Text Blocks

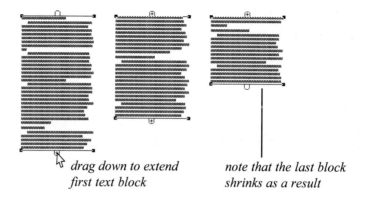

*drag down to extend
first text block*

*note that the last block
shrinks as a result*

As long as these blocks are linked by threaded text, changing one will affect the others.

Closing a Text Block

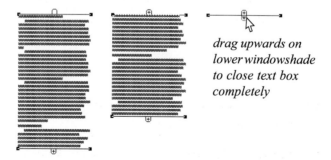

*drag upwards on
lower windowshade
to close text box
completely*

If you completely close a threaded text block (by dragging on a handle with the pointer tool), the text itself will not be destroyed - instead it will flow into the next block.

If the closed block was the last in the story, the previous block will contain a red triangle in its lower windowshade handle, giving you the chance to replace the text.

▷

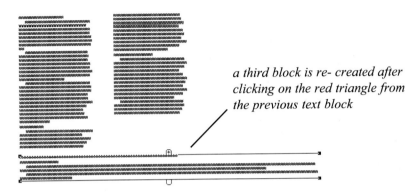

a third block is re- created after clicking on the red triangle from the previous text block

TIP

When placing a new text block, click-drag with the loaded text icon to predefine its width and size.

You can reflow text at any point:

1.   Click on a + sign on one of the existing blocks. The loaded text icon will appear, which gives you the opportunity to place the text from that point onwards in the story (note this will affect later text blocks which currently form part of the story).

2.   Click or click-drag to place the remaining text. You can abort this action by clicking on the pointer tool.

NOTE

Text is often threaded through blocks on consecutive pages.

Summary

A complete **Story** may be imported using the Place command, and may occupy several threaded text blocks.

A text block has **windowshade** handles, which give an indication as to how the text is threaded:

An empty windowshade handle denotes the end of a story.

A red triangle reminds you that there is more text still to be placed.

A plus sign (+) indicates that the story is continued to/from another existing text block.

TIP

To "de-thread" a text block, select with the pointer tool, choose Cut (Edit menu), then paste. The block will return as an independent text element.

Autoflow

1. Make sure that the Autoflow option is active (Layout menu).

2. Go to the File menu, and place a text file in the normal way. This time your loaded text icon will look like this:

3. Locate the position for the first text block and click once. PageMaker will place this block and then automatically generate all the additional text blocks according to the margins and column guides which are present. New pages will be created if required.

Keyboard Shortcuts

 Normal manual text-flow (default setting).

 Autoflow: hold down the **Control** key.

 Semi-Automatic flow: hold down **Control** and **Shift** together. With this option you still need to click to position each text block, but it is not necessary to click each red triangle.

CHAPTER

8

Master Pages

This chapter covers...

Master Pages

Column Guides

Master Pages

The Page icon labelled R represents the document master page. In a double-sided document there are two master pages labelled L and R (representing Left and Right pages).

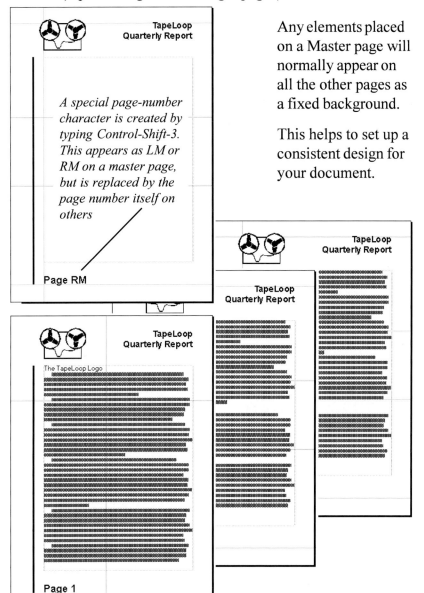

A special page-number character is created by typing Control-Shift-3. This appears as LM or RM on a master page, but is replaced by the page number itself on others

Any elements placed on a Master page will normally appear on all the other pages as a fixed background.

This helps to set up a consistent design for your document.

TIP

On individual document pages, you can switch off the Master items from the Layout menu.

NOTE

Although master elements are fixed (non-editable) on other pages, guidelines from a master page are. If you change them, however, you can reset them to their original state with Copy master guides (also from the Layout menu).

Column Guides

You can instruct PageMaker to automatically format pages with multiple columns of text.

1. Choose **Column guides** from the Layout menu. The following dialog box will appear:

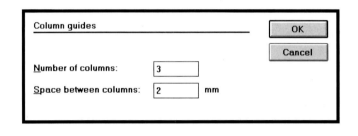

2. Enter the number of columns required and the space between them.

When you return to the page, these guides will appear dark blue. They are magnetic (like other guides). In addition when placing text you will find that it flows into a column rather than completely over the page.

Irregular Columns

1. Create the required number of columns using the previous method. They will initially be of equal width.

2. Manually drag the blue column boundaries left or right using the pointer tool. It may help to have the Control palette active, as you will be able to read off the Y coordinate as you move.

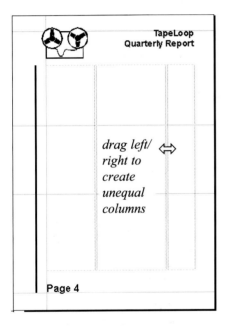

NOTE

Normally the guides and columns are set up on the Master page(s). This lets you set up a consistent layout all the way through the document.

CHAPTER

Working with Large Amounts of Text

This chapter covers...

Type Specifications

Paragraph Specifications

Widows and Orphans

The Keep With
Command

Column and Page Breaks

Paragraph Rules

Indents/Tabs

Hyphenation

Inline Graphics

Text Wrap

Type Specifications

Virtually all the text effects found in the Control palette are also accessible from the Type menu:

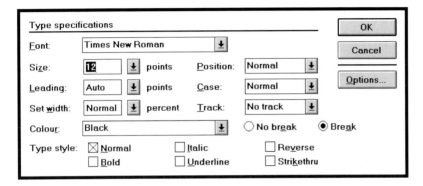

1.   Select the text you want to change.

2.   Choose **Type specs** from the Type menu. Virtually all the character level text attributes are present.

3.   The **Options** button allows you to customise the SMALL CAPS size as well as ^{Superscript} and $_{Subscript}$.

Paragraph Specifications

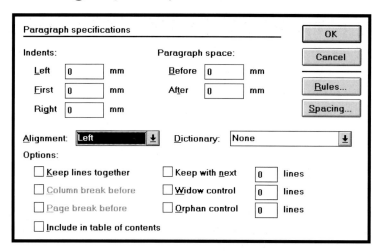

1. Either click an insertion point within the paragraph you want to change, or select multiple paragraphs with the Text tool.

2. Choose **Paragraph** from the Type menu.

3. All the paragraph level attributes can be accessed from this dialog box, e.g. space above/below, indents, alignment. The other attributes will be discussed later in this chapter.

Dictionary

Your PageMaker installation will include UK dictionaries, but you can also purchase additional dictionary files. These are used for spell checking and hyphenation purposes. From this dialog box you can specify the dictionary to be used for each paragraph.

Widows and Orphans

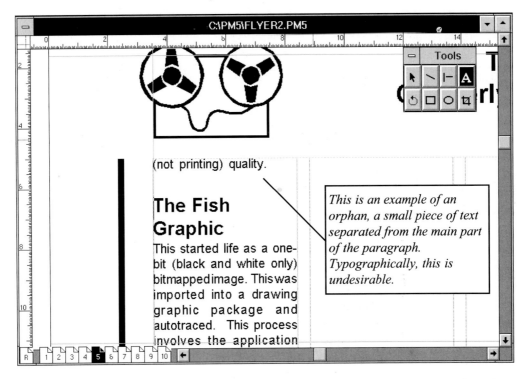

In the example below we are using the Paragraph dialog box to set orphan size to a minimum of 3 lines:

PageMaker will now automatically readjust textblocks so that no orphans of less than 3 lines appear:

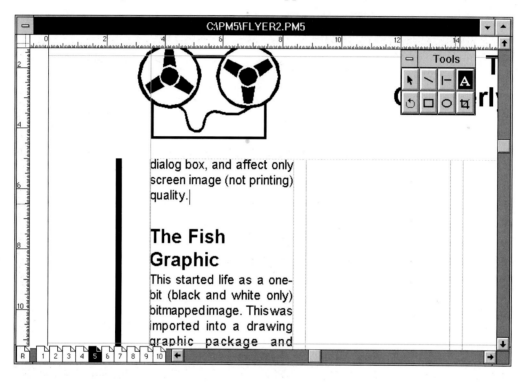

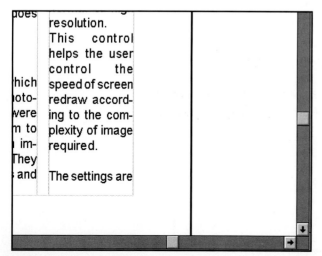

This is an example of a Widow, a similar problem where a small piece of text at the beginning of a paragraph is separated from the main text (Note: An Orphan leaves a small piece of text at the end of a paragraph block).

Widow control is also available from the Paragraph dialog box.

The Keep With Command

Sometimes we want to make sure that a paragraph such as a heading is kept with the next few lines, to avoid the following problem:

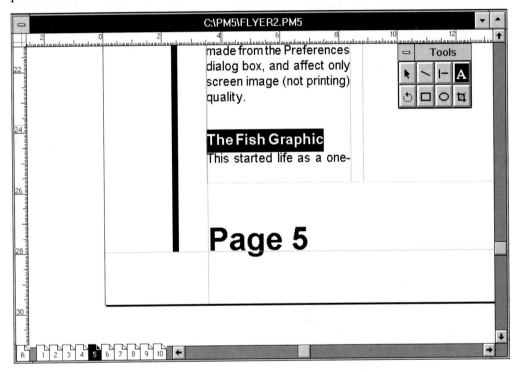

1. Select the heading paragraph.

2. Choose **Paragraph** from the Type menu.

3. To make sure the heading is kept with the next three lines of text (i.e. not broken over two columns or pages), enter 3 in the **Keep with** box. Click **OK**.

Column and Page Breaks

Sometimes we wish to ensure that there is always a column or page break before certain text paragraphs. In the example below we have set all three headings to include a column break, so each starts at the top of its own block:

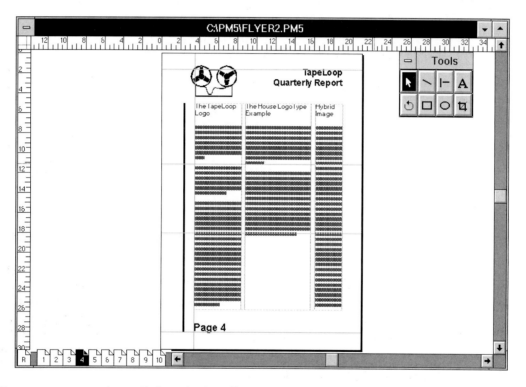

TIP

See chapter 11 "Style Sheets" for a more automatic way of setting these attributes to multiple headings.

1. Select the heading paragraph.

2. Choose **Paragraph** from the Type menu.

3. Set **Column break before**. Click **OK**.

4. Repeat for the other headings. From now on, no matter how you move or edit the text, PageMaker will always adjust the blocks so that each heading appears at the top of a column.

Paragraph Rules

Paragraph rules are lines directly above or below a paragraph. Unlike normal horizontal lines, they are attached to the text itself.

Creating

1. Select the required paragraph with the Text tool.

2. Choose **Paragraph** from the Type menu.

3. Click on the **Rules** button. The following dialog box will appear:

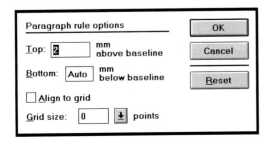

Here we are setting a 1 point green line to appear below the paragraph selected.

TIP

Although the measurement system is currently millimetres, you can enter other units into most dialog boxes. Points and picas are specified as in the following example:
3p6 represents 3 picas and 6 points (note 1 pica = 12 points).

4. Clicking on the **Options** button will allow you to specify how far above/below the baseline the rule should appear:

In the following example, these paragraph settings have been applied to the three centred headings:

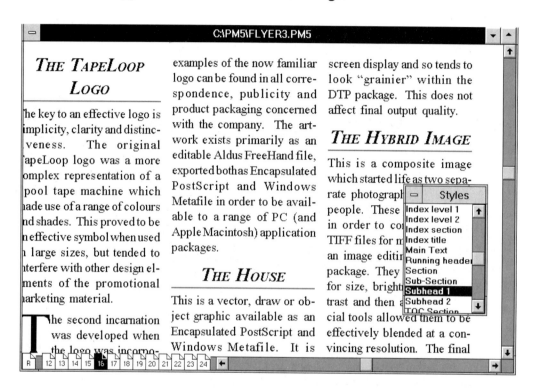

If this text is moved or edited, the paragraph rules too will move so that they are always in the correct position.

NOTE

Usually paragraph rules are used as part of a style definition. See Chapter 11 "Style Sheets" for more information.

Indents/Tabs

When entering text, the **Tab** key will move the insertion point to the next specified horizontal **Tab** position. It is useful to be able to specify your own tabulation:

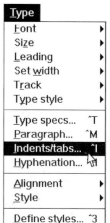

1. Select some text in which the **Tab** key has been used.

2. Choose **Indents/tabs** from the Type menu. The following ruler will appear in position above your text:

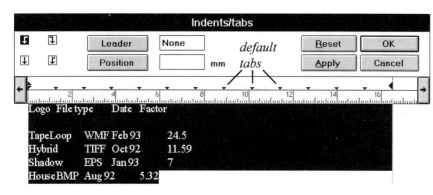

In the above example, the **Tab** key had been pressed once in between each item.

3. Click once above the ruler to create your own Tab marker. You can then select the type of Tab from the four Tab icons.

Tab icons:
left aligned,
right aligned,
centred and
decimal.

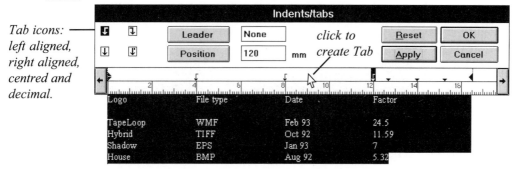

4. To see changes in the text without quitting the dialog box, click the **Apply** button.

In this example we created 3 left aligned Tabs at 4 cm intervals.
To move a Tab simply drag its icon left or right. To delete a Tab
drag it back down into the Ruler (it will disappear).

Setting leaders

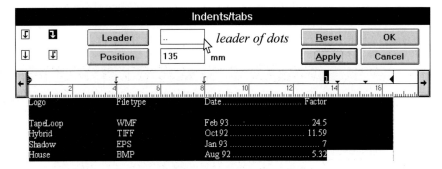

1.   Select a Tab by clicking directly on it.

2.   Choose a suitable symbol from the **Leader** pop-up menu.

3.   Click **Apply**.

In the example above, we have set a leader of dots which fill the
space leading up to the third Tab position.

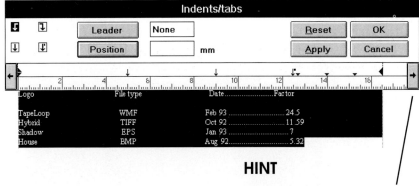

Above is an example of
centred and decimal Tabs.

HINT

*You can manually reposition the
ruler by dragging on its title bar.
The ruler itself has two scroll
icons which will move it left
and right.*

Setting Indents

The larger triangles at the sides of the ruler represent the left and right indents. (The left indent is split into first and subsequent paragraph lines). Although these are normally controlled numerically in the Paragraph dialog box, you can move them manually here by dragging.

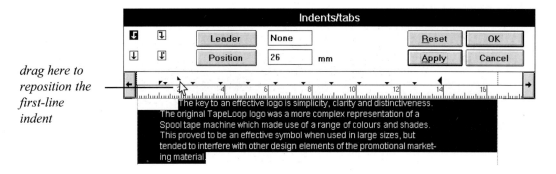

drag here to reposition the first-line indent

In this example we have set the first line indent to 26mm, the general left indent to 10mm, and the right indent to 30mm. These changes will be reflected in the Paragraph dialog box.

HINT

*By entering measurements in the box provided, and using the pop-up menu marked **Position**, you can add, delete and move tabs numerically rather than manually.*

Hyphenation

1.   Select the text you wish to change with the Text tool.

2.   Choose **Hyphenation** from the Type menu.

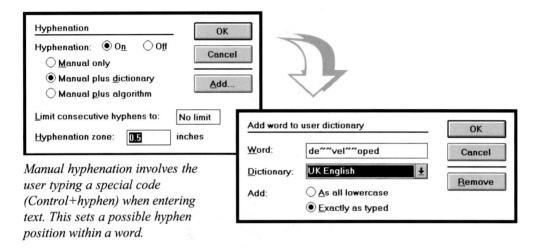

Manual hyphenation involves the user typing a special code (Control+hyphen) when entering text. This sets a possible hyphen position within a word.

NOTE

If a word is not present in PageMaker's hyphenation dictionary, it will use an intelligent algorithm to "guess" suitable positions for hyphens.

As well as switching hyphenation on and off, you can control the degree of hyphenation:-

Limit consecutive hyphens will allow you to set a limit to the number of consecutive lines which can end with hyphens.

Hyphenation zone is the width of text at the end of a line which PageMaker will consider for hyphenation.

PageMaker uses a hyphenation dictionary which contains markers within words at places where it is allowable to create a break.

Adding to the dictionary

1.   Select the word.

2.   Choose **Hyphenation** from the Type menu and click **Add**.

3.   Type the word using the tilda (~) to indicate possible hyphens. One tilda represents the most preferential break, two is less preferential and so on.

Inline Graphics

These are graphic elements which (like paragraph rules) are treated as part of a text block.

Placing

1.   With the Text tool, place an insertion point where you want the graphic to appear.

2.   Choose **Place** from the File menu.

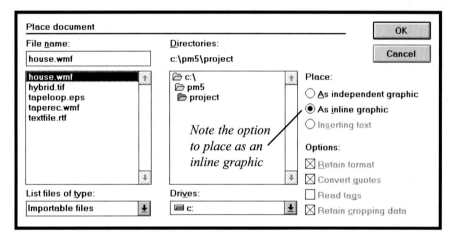

3.   Choose the graphic file, making sure the option to place as an inline graphic is active. If it is greyed out there is no insertion point active in your document, so you will need to repeat steps 1 and 2. Click **OK**.

4.   The graphic will appear as part of the text. It can still be resized with the Pointer tool, but to all other intents and purposes it is treated as a large character or text. This is very useful if you want an illustration to be kept with a certain piece of text even after radical editing at later stages.

Inline Graphic Example

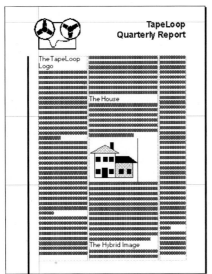

In this example a paragraph at the top of the first column was deleted.

Note how the inline graphic moves with the text...

Note that text effects such as centre alignment are also now available.

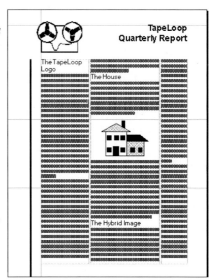

Changing an Inline Graphic to a Normal Graphic

1. Select the element with the Pointer tool.

2. From the Edit menu, choose **Cut** then **Paste**.

The graphic will return as a normal element free from the text block.

Changing a Normal Graphic to an Inline Graphic

1. Select the element with the Pointer tool.

2. Choose **Cut** from the Edit menu.

3. Select the Text tool and create an insertion point at the desired location within a text block.

4. Choose **Paste**.

The graphic will appear as part of the text block.

Text Wrap

This is used to prevent graphics and text from overlapping each other. It is applied to a graphic element to create a text-exclusion boundary.

Graphic with no wrap selected.

Regular Wrap

1. Select the graphic.

2. Choose **Text wrap** from the Element menu. The following dialog box will appear:

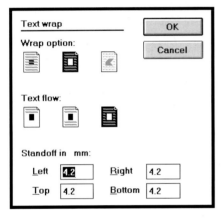

This graphic has a text wrap boundary (represented by the dotted line).

The three wrap options are:

> *no wrap (normal)*
> *regular wrap*
> *irregular wrap*

You can also choose whether you want text to flow above, above and below, or all around the graphic element

3. Currently No wrap is selected. Click on the second option, which allows text to wrap around a regular (rectangle) object.

4. Select the type of text flow required, usually the third option (text flowing all around the graphic).

5. Enter the standoff distance for each side. Click **OK**.

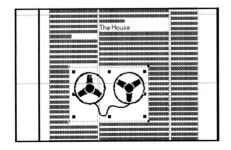

If you now move the graphic over some text, the text will reflow around it at the agreed distance.

Irregular Wrap

You can create an irregular text wrap by manually editing the exclusion zone around a regularly wrapped graphic.

1.   As before, create a regular wrap around the graphic.

2.   Zoom in so that you can see the dotted line clearly. The line joins small diamond shaped handles, which can be manually dragged about with the pointer tool.

Click on a vacant part of the dotted line to create a new "handle"

Drag a handle in order to edit the boundary into an irregular shape

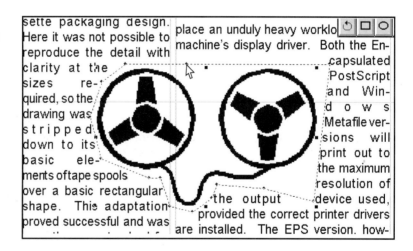

TIP

If screen redraw is slow during editing of the boundary, hold down the spacebar. The text will not reflow until you release.

If you now return to the Text wrap dialog box, you will see that the irregular wrap option (previously greyed out), is now active.

CHAPTER 10

The Story Editor

This chapter covers...

The Story Editor

Features of the Story
Editor

Story and Layout Views

The Story Editor

The Story Editor provides you with a simplified view of text, with an entire story in one window (even if it is split into many text blocks in normal layout view).

Starting Up

1. Select the text to be edited.

2. Choose **Edit story** from the Edit menu.

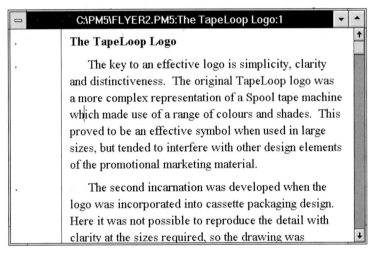

For convenience and fast editing purposes, the story is displayed in one font and one size. The subtler text effects are not shown.

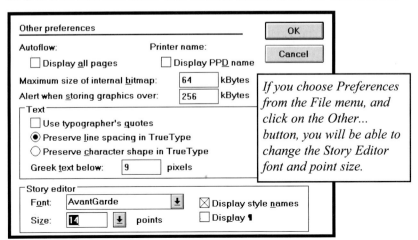

If you choose Preferences from the File menu, and click on the Other... button, you will be able to change the Story Editor font and point size.

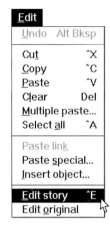

TIP

Another way to call up the Story editor is to triple-click on a text block with the Pointer tool.

Features of the Story Editor

The Spelling Checker

1. From the Story editor, choose Spelling from the Utilities menu. The following dialog box will appear:

Spelling
Unknown word : effectivley
Change to: effectivley
effectively / afflictively / effective / affective / effectivity
Ignore / Replace / Add...
Options: ⊠ Alternate spellings   ⊠ Show duplicates
Search document: ● Current publication   ○ All publications
Search story: ○ Selected text   ● Current story   ○ All stories

2. Choose whether you want to check the entire document, the current story, or just a sample of text which you have selected.

3. Click the **Start** button.

PageMaker will warn you of any words it cannot locate in its dictionary. If the word is indeed incorrect then you have the choice to re-enter it or choose from a selection of closest matches in the Dictionary. If the word is correct (e.g. a proper noun) then you can instruct PageMaker either to ignore this occurrence or to add it to the user section of the dictionary.

The Spell checker will also warn you about duplicate words (a common typing mistake), and possible capitalisation errors.

4. When the Spell check is complete, close the Spelling window to return to the main part of the Story editor.

▷

Find and Change

These are both options in the Utilities menu. You can search a story for specific text or attributes, and automatically replace any instances with different words or effects.

1. Choose **Change** from the Utilities menu.

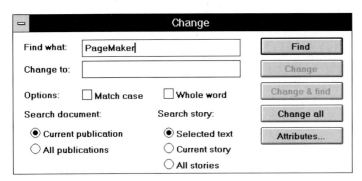

2. You can now enter the search text, and text which will replace this. You can also search/replace on attributes by clicking the **Attributes** button. In this example we shall look for all instances of the word PageMaker, changing them to Bold.

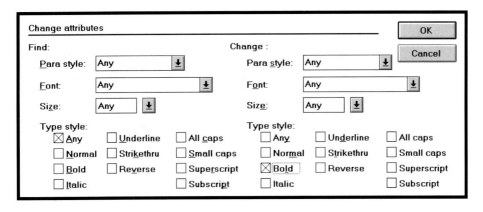

3.   You can manually step through the search (using the **Find next** and **Change** buttons) or click on **Change all** to instruct PageMaker to carry out the task automatically.

4.   When finished, close the Change window to return to the main Story view. The result can be seen below:

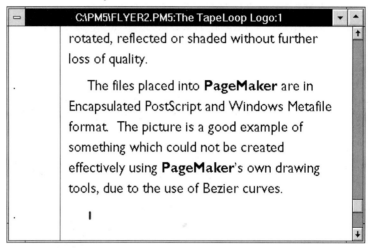

The **Find** function works in exactly the same way (but without the facility to replace text). It is also possible to search/replace using the following metacharacters:

(The ^ symbol means that you should hold down the Control key)			
		Section marker	^6
		Paragraph marker	^7
		Registermark symbol	^r
		Caret	^^
Wildcard character	^?	White space	^w
Carriage return	^p	Thin space	^<
Line break	^n	Non-breaking space	^s
Tab	^t	En space	^>
Discretionary (soft) hyphen	^-	Em space	^m
Nonbreaking hyphen	^~	En dash	^=
Computer-inserted hyphen	^c	Em dash	^_
In-line graphic marker	^g	Nonbreaking slash	^/
Index marker	^;	Single open quote	^[
Page # marker	^3	Single close quote	^]
Bullet	^8	Double open quote	^{
Copyright symbol	^2	Double close quote	^}

Story and Layout Views

You can return to Layout view (pages and pasteboard) from the Edit menu, or by closing down the Story window.

In PageMaker you can operate many story windows which can be arranged, minimised, maximised or resized in the normal way.

In the example below we have several documents open simultaneously: their layout windows have been minimised so that we can easily choose which document or story to select.

NOTE

Invoking the Story editor with no text selected will open up a new story. You will be asked to place this on leaving the Story editor.

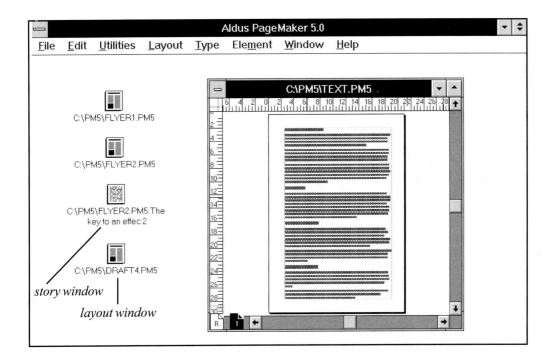

NOTE

In the Story editor you still have access to the Type menu, and with it the full range of PageMaker text effects. Remember however that you will not see many of the changes until you return to the Layout view.

Display Invisible Characters

1.   Choose **Preferences** from the File menu.

2.   Click on **Other**.

Note the option to display normally invisible characters in the Story editor. It is often useful to be able to visually distinguish between spaces, tabs and return characters.

11

Style
Sheets

This chapter covers...

Paragraph Styles

Using Styles

Changing a Style

Style by Example

Copying Styles from
another Document

Paragraph Styles

Styles allow you to save a complete set of text attributes under a single name, which you can then use quickly and easily throughout your documents.

Defining a style

1. Choose **Define styles** from the Type menu. The following dialog box will appear:

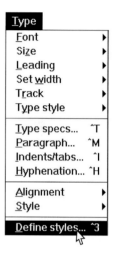

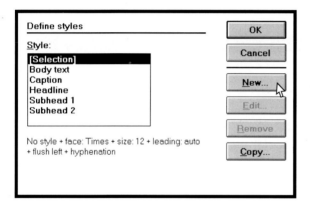

2. Click on **New** to create a new style.

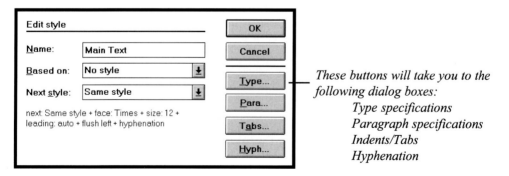

These buttons will take you to the following dialog boxes:
Type specifications
Paragraph specifications
Indents/Tabs
Hyphenation

3. Enter a name for the style, then use the **Type**, **Para**, **Tabs** and **Hyph** buttons to set the text attributes.

4. Click **OK** when you have finished.

Using Styles

1.   Make sure the Styles palette is active (Window menu).

2.   With the Text tool, select or click inside the paragraph you want to change.

3.   Click on the appropriate style in the palette. The style, along with all its attributes, will be applied to the text. In this example, the style Subhead1 has been applied to all subheadings on the page:

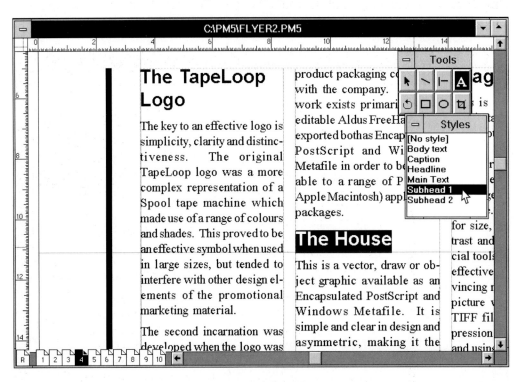

Changing a Style

1. Choose **Define styles** from the Type menu.

2. Click on the style you wish to change, then on the **Edit** button.

3. Make the changes to the attributes. If you hold down **Shift** when clicking **OK** PageMaker will exit from all dialog boxes (even if you are several levels inside).

PageMaker remembers the style applied to each paragraph, so in this example all the Subhead1 paragraphs change instantly.

TIP

A shortcut to Edit a style is to hold down the Control key and click directly on the style name within the palette.

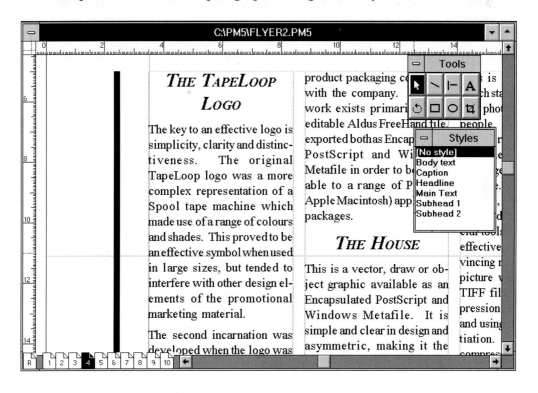

Style by Example

Sometimes it is useful to be able to experiment with text effects directly on the page, so that you can test out ideas before deciding on the exact attributes for your styles. Once you have done this, you can sample the text to automatically create a style definition.

Let us assume that you have a specimen piece of text which already has all the attributes you would like to build into a style.

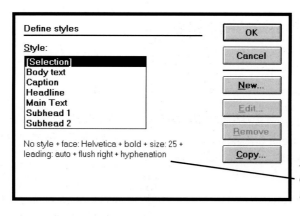

1.   Select part of the text. Note that **[no style]** is highlighted in the Styles palette.

2.   Choose **Define styles** from the Type menu.

PageMaker is aware of all the attributes of the selected text

3.   Making sure that **[Selection]** is active, click on **New.**

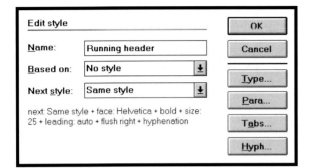

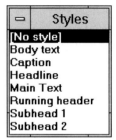

the new style will now appear in the palette...

4. Enter a name for the Style. All the attributes of the selected text are already present, so there is no more work to be done. Hold down **Shift** and click **OK** to return to the page.

Styles in the Story Editor

You can also use the Style palette in the Story editor. Since many text effects do not show up in a Story window, Style names appear in the margin to help you keep track of current settings.

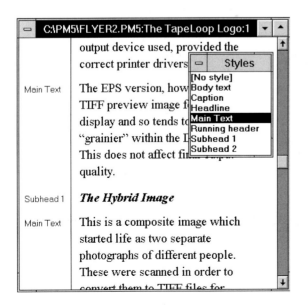

HINT

The facility to display style names in the margin of a Story window can be turned on and off from the Other Preferences dialog box.

To reach this, choose Preferences from the File menu, then click Other.

Copying Styles from another Document

1.   Choose **Define styles** from the Type menu.

2.   Click on the **Copy** button.

3.   Locate the document and click **OK**.

If this document uses the same style names you will be asked if you wish to overwrite existing styles.

HINT

If you close all documents you can change the global default Styles.

CHAPTER

12

Colour

This chapter covers...

The Colour Palette

Creating New Colours

Importing Colours

Colour Libraries

The Colour Palette

Using Colours

1. Make sure the Colour palette is active (Window menu).

2. Select an element.

3. Choose whether you want to alter the fill colour, line colour, or both (use the pop-up menu in the palette).

The Colour palette

NOTE

Some imported elements may use their own colour information and will, therefore, be unaffected by the Colour palette.

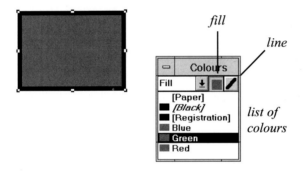

4. Click on the required colour in the palette.

Changing Text Colour

1. Select the text with the Text tool.

2. Apply the colour from the palette.

Creating New Colours

Spot Colours

If you are printing using a colour printer, then you will probably want all colours to be reproduced on a composite page.

However, it is more usual when producing longer print-runs to separate colours. A spot colour will appear on a separate sheet of its own, so that it may be reproduced using a specially mixed printer's ink.

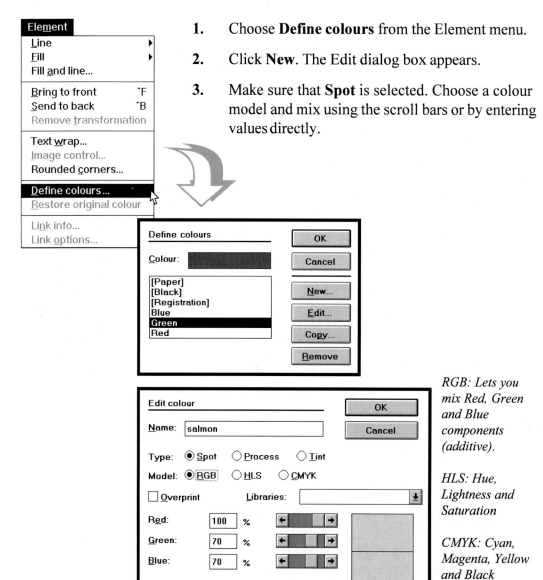

Element
Line   ▶
Fill   ▶
Fill and line...

Bring to front   ˆF
Send to back   ˆB
Remove transformation

Text wrap...
Image control...
Rounded corners...

Define colours...   °
Restore original colour

Link info...
Link options...

Define colours   OK

Colour: [   ]   Cancel

[Paper]
[Black]   New...
[Registration]
Blue   Edit...
Green
Red   Copy...

                                       Remove

Edit colour   OK

Name: [salmon   ]   Cancel

Type: ◉ Spot   ○ Process   ○ Tint

Model: ◉ RGB   ○ HLS   ○ CMYK

☐ Overprint   Libraries: [   ] ↕

Red: [100] %   ◀ [   ] ▶
Green: [70]   %   ◀ [   ] ▶
Blue: [70]   %   ◀ [   ] ▶

1. Choose **Define colours** from the Element menu.

2. Click **New**. The Edit dialog box appears.

3. Make sure that **Spot** is selected. Choose a colour model and mix using the scroll bars or by entering values directly.

RGB: Lets you mix Red, Green and Blue components (additive).

HLS: Hue, Lightness and Saturation

CMYK: Cyan, Magenta, Yellow and Black (subtractive).

4. Enter a name for the new colour.

5. When you return to the page the new colour will appear in the palette.

▷

Process Colours

Process colours are not printed on their own separate sheet. Instead they contribute to 4 process separations by dividing into Cyan, Magenta, Yellow and Black components. This way you can use an unlimited number of colours without worrying about the cost of many separations.

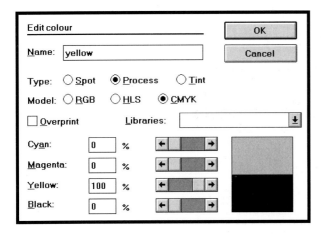

Process selected under Colour type.

NOTE

Although it is normal to define process colours using CMYK, PageMaker will let you use whichever colour model you prefer. You can even switch colour models as you edit.

Editing Colours

1. Choose **Define colours** from the Element menu.

2. Select the colour and click **Edit**.

3. Make the necessary changes then click **OK**.

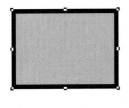

Any elements already using this colour will automatically change.

TIP

As with styles, a quick way to edit is to Control-click directly on the colour name in the palette.

Importing Colours

In this example, the House picture was imported from Aldus FreeHand (a graphics package). It is a colour image which made use of the colours "orange" and "purple". When the graphic was placed, these spot colours were imported as well, and appeared in the colour palette.

This means that they are available to be used by other PageMaker elements.

Colour Libraries

When using the **Edit colour** dialog box, you can select a predefined colour from any of the standard libraries:

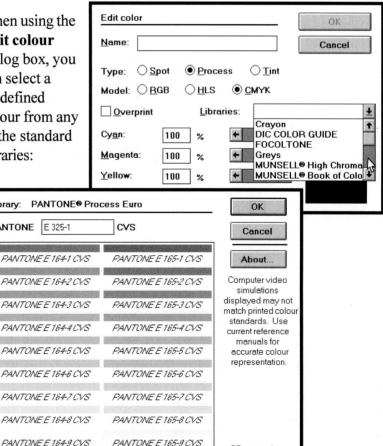

CHAPTER

13

Aldus
Additions

This chapter covers...

Additions	Pub Info
Sort Pages	Story/Textblock Info
Traverse Textblocks	Drop Cap
Contination Line	Edit Tracks
Balance Columns	Expert Kerning
Build Booklet	Open Template
Create Colour Library	PS Group-It/Ungroup-It
Create Keyline	Other Additions

Additions

Additions are utility modules which can be added to PageMaker by third party developers. In this book we shall look at some of the Additions which are included in PageMaker version 5.

The Additions Submenu

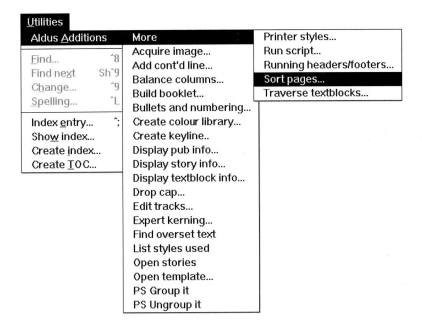

NOTE

As more Additions are produced, these menus will grow.

Additions exist as .add files within an Addition directory, which is itself a subdirectory of the Aldus directory. It is therefore easy to add or remove additions as they become available, without having to disturb the installation of PageMaker.

Sort Pages

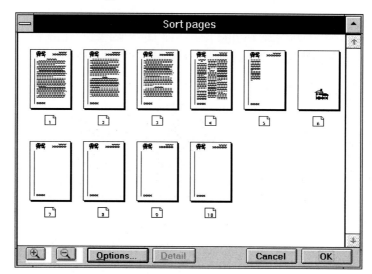

This Addition allows you to easily re-order the pages in your document, simply by dragging the page thumbnail images around within the Sort window.

This is a very powerful and drastic operation to perform, so you are advised to save your document before proceeding.

Traverse Textblocks

1.   Select a text block which is part of a threaded story.

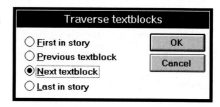

2.   Choose **Traverse textblocks** from the Additions submenu.

3.   Choose from the first, previous, subsequent or last textblock in the threaded story, and click **OK**.

PageMaker will automatically locate the desired textblock.

Continuation Line

1. Select a piece of text which is threaded to another page.

2. Choose **Continuation line** from the Additions submenu.

PageMaker locates the page of the previous/next textblock, and automatically creates the Continued from/to message and line.

The size of the existing textblock will be adjusted to accommodate this.

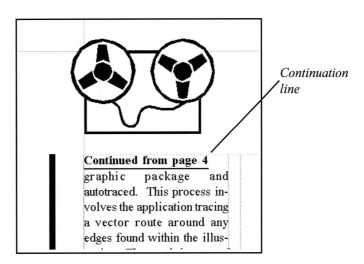

Continuation line

Continued from page 4
graphic   package   and autotraced. This process involves the application tracing a vector route around any edges found within the illus-

Balance Columns

This should be used when you have a story threaded through several columns of text, and wish to balance them so that they are of equal vertical height.

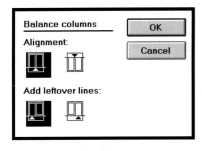

1. Select the threaded text blocks.

2. Choose **Balance columns** from the Additions submenu.

3. Set the alignment option.

4. Sometimes it is not possible to balance exactly, so choose whether you want leftover lines in the left or right column.

5. Click **OK**.

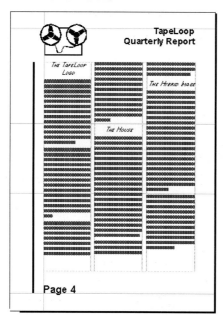

Example of balanced columns

Build Booklet

This provides an element of page imposition for PageMaker.

If your printer's page size is large enough, it may be possible to print several pages of a document at once. Build Booklet allows you to control the order and orientation of these pages.

| Build booklet | | (e163) | OK |

Publication: C:\PM5\FLYER3.PM5   Cancel

Spread size: [421]   x   [298]   millimeters

Page 5
Page 6
Page 7
Page 8
Page 9
Page 10
Page 11
blank page

[Blank page]   Layout: [2-up saddle stitch ▼]

[Invert pages]   Pages per group: [4 ▼]

[Delete]

[Revert]   ☐ Use creep

Total creep: [0]   millimeters

Gutter space: [0]   millimeters

Messages
Page count: 12

☒ Place guides in gutter

☒ Preserve page numbering

In this example, when printing a booklet two pages at a time, we would like the front and back cover (i.e. the first and last page) to be printed together. Likewise the second and the penultimate page should be together.

Selecting 2-up saddle stitch will create this effect. Note that our document has 11 pages, an odd number. To print pages in twos it is necessary to add a blank page.

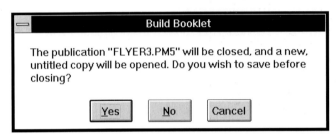

PageMaker creates a new document with the large pages, each containing two pages from the original document.

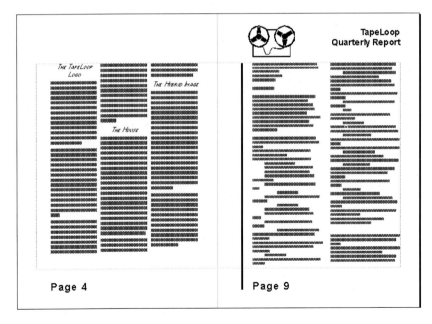

NOTE

The new document is intended for printing purposes only.
Any editing should be carried out on the original.

Create Colour Library

This Addition reads the items in your current colour palette, and uses them to create a new colour library.

You define the library name, the disk file name used and also the number of columns and rows. You can also enter text notes (this will be displayed when the **About** button is used).

Create colour library

| Library name: | TapeLoop |
| File name: | CUSTOM1|BCF |

Save
Cancel
Browse...

Preferences:

Colours per column: 5

Colours per row: 3

Notes:

TapeLoop Corporate Scheme
Specified June 1993

In this example a corporate colour library is created which can now be used in any other PageMaker document.

This is how the new library appears, accessible (like the standard libraries) from the Edit colour dialog box.

Library: TapeLoop

orange

OK
Cancel
About...

Red	purple
Green	orange
Blue	PANTONE E 325-1
salmon	
yellow	

Computer video simulations displayed may not match printed colour standards. Use current reference manuals for accurate colour representation.

Create Keyline

This draws a box around a selected element, either directly over it or at a specified border distance.

The Attributes button gives you the opportunity to set the fill and line attributes of the box.

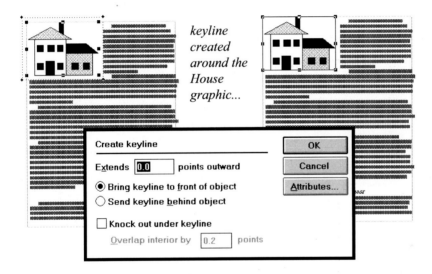

keyline created around the House graphic...

Pub Info

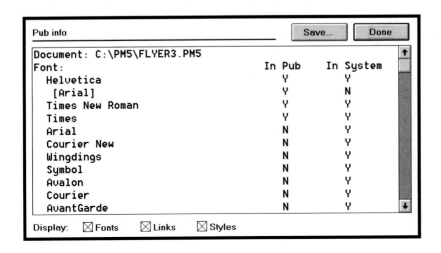

Pub Info

Rather than telling you about recommended local drinking establishments, this Addition gives you a complete listing of the fonts, text styles, and imported graphics used in your document.

Story/Textblock Info

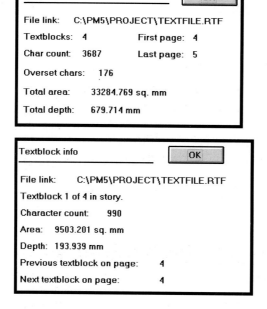

This produces statistics for the currently selected story.

This produces statistics for the currently selected textblock.

Drop Cap

1.   Select a paragraph and choose **Drop cap** from the Additions submenu.

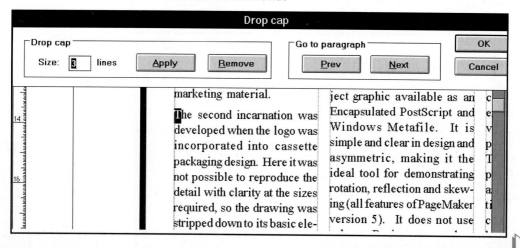

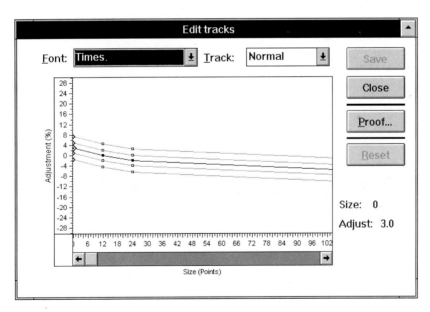

2. Enter the number of lines over which the initial capital letter should appear.

3. Click **OK**.

This Addition creates a drop capital by editing the Type specs of the first letter in the paragraph and inserting tab characters to move the rest of the text out of the way.

It is therefore important to also use the Addition to remove a drop cap, as it will clear away these extra effects automatically.

The second incarnation was developed when the logo was incorporated into cassette packaging design. Here it was not possible to reproduce the detail with clarity at the sizes required, so the drawing was stripped down to its basic ele-

Edit Tracks

You can use this Addition to edit the tracking algorithm for different fonts. Note that there are five algorithms to edit, ranging from **Very loose** to **Very tight**.

To help visualise the effects of the tracking algorithms, click on the **Proof** button. This instructs PageMaker to automatically generate a document demonstrating tracking at different point sizes:

Create proof sheet for Times

Create

Cancel

Tracks:

⊠ Very loose
⊠ Loose
⊠ Normal
⊠ Tight
⊠ Very tight

Font sizes:

8
10
11
12
14
18
24

For 8 pt use:

○ Short text
● Long text

Add size...

Remove size

Short sample text: Short sample

Long sample text: This is sample text for Edit tracks. This should be enough text to represent this typeface in this track and in this size.

and in this size.
Normal 12.0 point Times
This is sample text for Edit tracks. This should be enough text to represent this typeface in this track and in this size.
Tight 12.0 point Times
This is sample text for Edit tracks. This should be enough text to represent this typeface in this track and in this size.
Very Tight 12.0 point Times
This is sample text for Edit tracks. This should be enough text to represent this typeface in this track and in this size.
Very Loose 14.0 point Times
This is sample text for Edit tracks. This should be enough text to

Part of the example proofing document, demonstrating tracking algorithms for a range of sizes using the Times font.

Expert Kerning

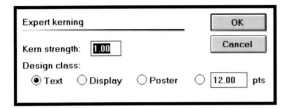

This Addition removes all manual kerning from the selected text, and instead applies its own intelligent pair kerning.

The design class option you use depends on the design purpose of the font (if in doubt about this, select Text).

NOTE

You should switch off automatic pair kerning (Spacing from the Paragraph dialog box) before using this Addition.

Open Template

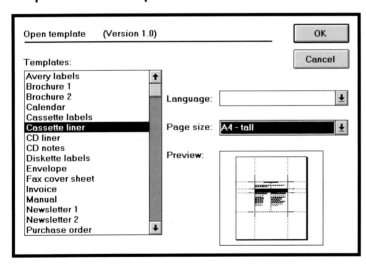

This Addition automatically generates Template PageMaker documents which you can adapt for your own use.

1.   Select **Open template** from the Additions submenu.

2.   Choose a design and page size.

When you click **OK** a new untitled document will take shape.

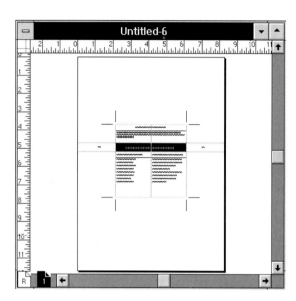

This is an example of the Cassette Liner template document.

PS Group-It/Ungroup-It

This is a useful Addition which takes multiple elements and transforms them into a single PostScript element.

1.   Select all the elements to be grouped (either by Shift-clicking or using a selection box).

2.   Choose **PS Group-It** from the Additions submenu.

Elements ready to be grouped.

The resulting element can now be resized, rotated or transformed in any way as a single unit.

Because PostScript is a printing language, the screen preview image may be cruder than the high-quality printed version.

To separate the elements once more, select and choose PS Ungroup-it from the Additions submenu.

Other Additions

Find Overset Text

This will locate any red triangles in the lower windowshade handle of text blocks (indicating text still to be placed within the document).

Open Stories

This will open all stories within the current document in the Story editor (up to a maximum of 10).

Run Script

Common tasks in PageMaker can be programmed using a special scripting language. This is essentially a list of commands stored in a text block or text file, which can then be automatically run using this Addition.

Printer Styles

This is discussed in Chapter 17 "Printing".

CHAPTER

14

The Table Editor

This chapter covers...

The Table Editor

Entering Text

Importing Text

Adjusting Table Dimensions

Grouping Cells

Changing Text Attributes

Lines

The Borders Command

Fills

Number Format

Saving and Exporting

Using a Table in PageMaker

Launching Table Editor
from PageMaker

The Table Editor

This is a separate Application program designed to help you create Tables of text for use in PageMaker.

Table Editor 2.1

Double click to launch the Table Editor from the Program Manager.

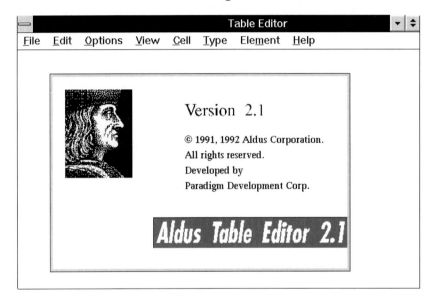

The Table Editor is very similar to PageMaker in operation.

Starting Off

1. Choose **New** from the File menu.

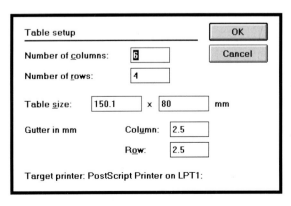

Choose the initial number of columns and rows for your table.

It is easy to change these settings later on.

Entering Text

1. Select the **Text** tool.

2. Click inside a cell to place an insertion point.

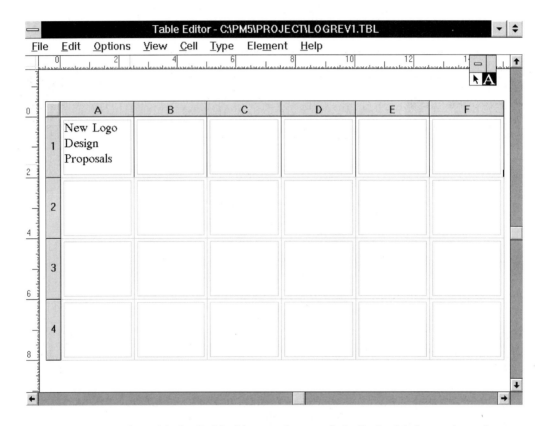

The table is divided into columns (labelled with letters), and rows (labelled with numbers). There are rulers, grid labels, and grid lines, all of which can be deactivated/reactivated from the Options menu.

The Toolbox contains only two items: the Text tool, and the Pointer (used to select multiple cells). Unlike PageMaker it is possible to change text attributes using either tool.

Importing Text

1. If you want to import text into part of the table only, select these cells with the pointer tool (drag to create a selection area).

2. Choose **Import** from the File menu.

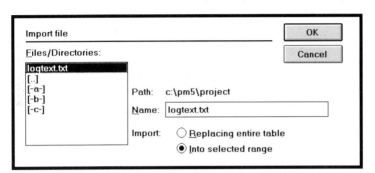

3. Select the required file and click **OK**.

The text will be read into the cells. The Table Editor can import text which uses Tab characters to indicate the division between cells. It can also export text in this form.

	A	B	C	D	E	F
1	New Logo Design Proposals					
2	Name	Type	File Size (bytes)	Version	Date	Used
3	TapeLoop	Windows Metafile	36056	7	Mar 92	35
4	Hybrid	Tagged Image File Format	21886	1	Sep 92	44

Adjusting Table Dimensions

On the Page

1.   Move into the grey grid label area.

2.   When your pointer is over a cell boundary line it will turn into a white double arrow. Drag left or right to resize the column (or up and down for a row).

drag to move cell boundaries

	A	B	C	D	E	F
1	New Logo Design Proposals					
2	Name	Type	File Size (bytes)	Version	Date	Used
3	TapeLoop	Windows Metafile	36056	7	Mar 92	35
4	Hybrid	Tagged Image File Format	21886	1	Sep 92	44

HINT

*Normally increasing the size of a row/column will be at the expense of the next row/column. If you hold down the **Alt** key, however, the Table size will increase as you move.*

This also applies when you are reducing a row or column.

Resizing the Grid Numerically

1. Select the row(s)/column(s) to be resized.

2. Choose **Column width** or **Row height** from the Cell menu.

Column width		OK
Column width:	20 mm	Cancel

3. Enter the width or height value. Click **OK**.

Grouping Cells

1. Select the cells to be grouped (using the pointer tool).

	A	B	C	D	E	F
1	New Logo Design Proposals					
2	Name	Type	File Size (bytes)	Version	Date	Used
3	TapeLoop	Windows Metafile	36056	7	Mar 92	35
4	Hybrid	Tagged Image File Format	21886	1	Sep 92	44

2. Choose **Group** from the Cell menu.

	A	B	C	D	E	F
1	New Logo Design Proposals					

TIP

You can select entire rows or columns by clicking on their grey grid label. If you click on the small grey square in the top left hand corner the complete table will be selected.

Changing Text Attributes

1. Select the text with either tool.

2. Choose **Type specs** from the Type menu. The following dialog box will appear:

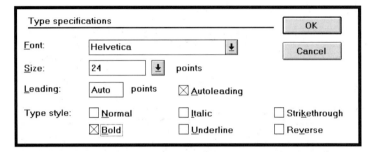

An interesting feature of the Table Editor is its ability to centre text (within each cell) both horizontally and vertically...

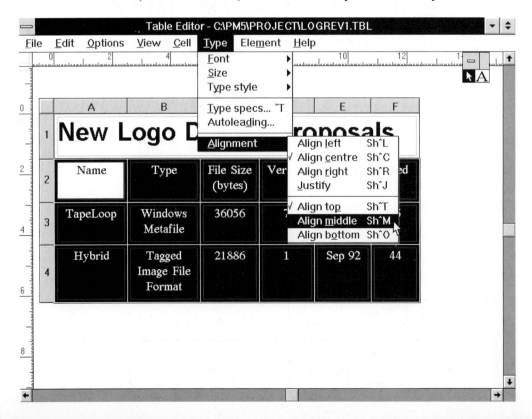

Lines

1. Select the cells to be changed.

2. Choose the required line style from the Lines submenu.

2 pt lines

The Borders Command

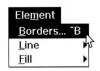

Normally line changes affect all lines within a selection. If you want to change only certain lines choose **Borders**.

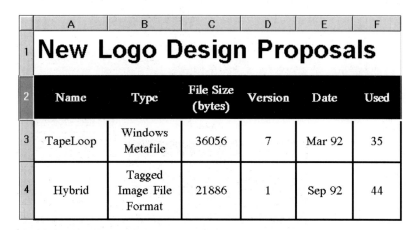

In this example we have switched off all checkboxes apart from "Verticals". This means that the new 2pt line style will only be applied to the vertical lines in the interior of the selected cells.

This is the result...

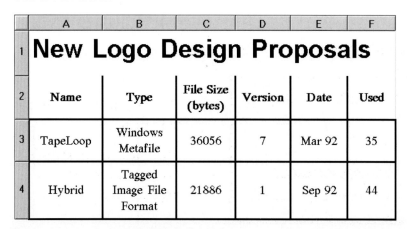

Fills

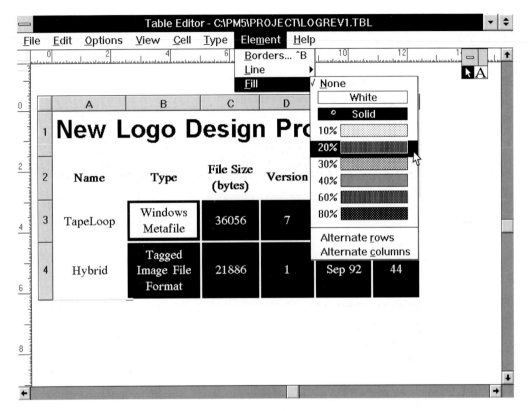

1. Select the cells to be filled.

2. Choose the required option from Fills (in the Element menu).

Number Format

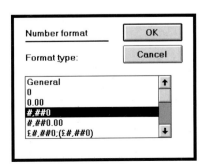

This option can be found in the cell menu.

The effect of this setting can be seen on the next page...

◁

*The finished
table* ——————

New Logo Design Proposals

Name	Type	File Size (bytes)	Version	Date	Used
TapeLoop	Windows Metafile	36,056	7	Mar 92	35
Hybrid	Tagged Image File Format	21,886	1	Sep 92	44

Saving and Exporting

The **Save** option (File menu) saves the document as a .tbl file.
This can be re-opened for editing, and is also a placeable
document in PageMaker.

Alternatively, you can export the table as a Windows Metafile
(**Export** from the File menu):

NOTE

*You can also
export as tab-
delimited text.*

Export to file   OK

Directories: Cancel

[.]
[-a-]   Path: c:\pm5\project
[-b-]
[-c-]   Name:

                   Export: ◉ Entire table
                              ○ Selected cell range

File format:

Windows Metafile
Text only (tab delimited)

Using a Table in PageMaker

Back in PageMaker, use the **Place** command (File menu) to import the Table as a normal graphic element.

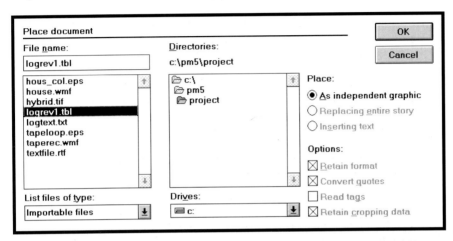

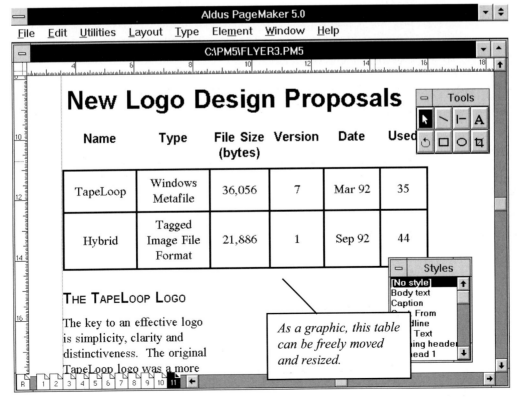

As a graphic, this table can be freely moved and resized.

Launching Table Editor from PageMaker

There is a dynamic link between PageMaker and the Table Editor.

To Edit a Table from PageMaker

1. Locate the table in the PageMaker document.

2. Hold down the **Alt** key and double-click on the table. The Table Editor will be sublaunched.

3. Carry out the necessary changes in the Table Editor.

4. Exit the Table Editor, saving changes (File menu). You will be returned to PageMaker, viewing the modified table.

NOTE

If the changes are not immediately reflected in the PageMaker document, this may be because the "hot link", has been turned off. See the next chapter for information about links.

Links
Management

This chapter covers...

The Links Dialog Box

Link Status

Object Linking using Windows

The Links Dialog Box

1. Choose **Links** from the File menu.

The following dialog box appears. This gives you information about all items of text and graphics which have been placed into your document:

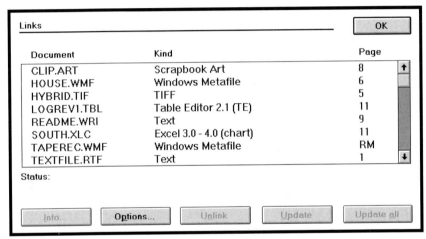

PageMaker keeps track of all imported elements, remembering their file type, size, location and date modified.

2. Select an item from the list and click the **Info** button.

Full details of the item appear:

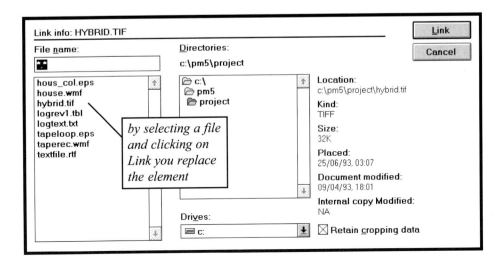

by selecting a file and clicking on Link you replace the element

3.   Click **Cancel** to return to the Links dialog box. Select
      another element and click on **Options**:

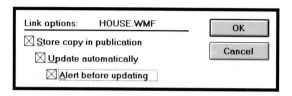

For graphic elements you have a choice to store the copy within
the publication. This tends to make your document size large, but
it also means that everything required for printing is available in
this single file.

By setting automatic updates, you create a hot link. This means
that whenever the source document is modified, PageMaker will
re-import so that it always works with the most up-to-date
version.

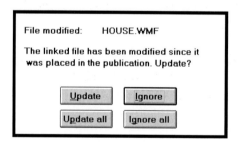

*If you set the Alert before
updating option, this
message will appear
whenever PageMaker
attempts to update a link.*

You can also access Link info and Link options directly from
your document:

1.   Select the element with the Pointer tool.

2.   Choose **Link info** or **Link options** from the Element
      menu.

Link Status

Sometimes a symbol appears next to items in the Links dialog:

```
┌─────────────────────────────────────────────────────────────┐
│  Links                                          ┌──────────┐  │
│  ─────────────────────────────────────────      │    OK    │  │
│                                                 └──────────┘  │
│      Document           Kind                    Page         │
│    ┌─────────────────────────────────────────────────┐ ┌─┐  │
│    │ CLIP.ART          Scrapbook Art            8    │ │▲│  │
│    │? HOUSE.WMF        Windows Metafile         6    │ ├─┤  │
│    │- HYBRID.TIF       TIFF                     5    │ │ │  │
│    │  LOGREV1.TBL      Table Editor 2.1 (TE)    11   │ │ │  │
│    │  README.WRI       Text                     9    │ │ │  │
│    │  SOUTH.XLC        Excel 3.0 - 4.0 (chart)  11   │ │ │  │
│    │  TAPEREC.WMF      Windows Metafile         RM   │ │ │  │
│    │  TEXTFILE.RTF     Text                     1    │ │▼│  │
│    └─────────────────────────────────────────────────┘ └─┘  │
│  Status:  The linked file has been modified since the last time it was placed. │
│           However, updates have not been requested.          │
│  ┌───────┐ ┌──────────┐ ┌────────┐ ┌────────┐ ┌──────────┐  │
│  │ Info... │ │ Options...│ │ Unlink │ │ Update │ │Update all│  │
│  └───────┘ └──────────┘ └────────┘ └────────┘ └──────────┘  │
└─────────────────────────────────────────────────────────────┘
```

The hyphen (-) indicates that the item has been modified, and that automatic updating was not requested. This means that the PageMaker version is now out of date. You can remedy this by clicking on **Update**.

The question mark tells you that PageMaker can no longer locate the original file. You can reset the link by clicking on **Info**, or choose to clear the link completely by clicking on **Unlink**.

Object Linking using Windows

As we have seen, PageMaker uses its own Links management system. We can also use the dynamic linking features of the Microsoft Windows operating system.

An Example

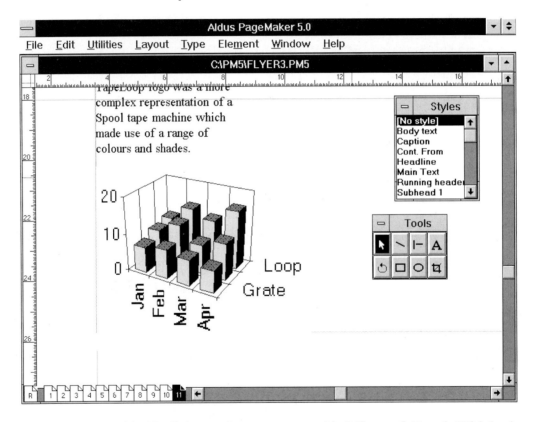

This 3D Column chart was created in Microsoft Excel. With both Excel and PageMaker running, the chart was selected, copied (using Excel's Edit menu), then pasted (using PageMaker's Edit menu).

Updates to the original Excel document will be automatically reflected in the PageMaker publication.

CHAPTER

Long Document Features

This chapter covers...

The Book Command

Table of Contents (TOC)

Rebuilding the TOC

Indexing

Creating the Index

The Book Command

When working with a long publication, it is common practice to divide it amongst several PageMaker documents. You can still treat these as a single publication using the Book command.

1. Choose **Book** from the File menu.

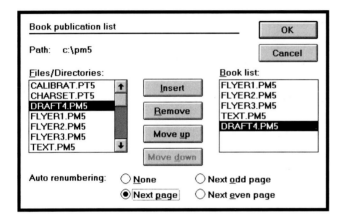

2. Locate each component file, using the **Insert** button to add them to the Book list.

3. Use the **Move up** and **Move down** buttons to assemble the "chapters" in the correct order.

4. Select the appropriate type of Page numbering. Click **OK**.

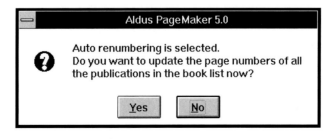

NOTE

Choosing auto renumbering will cause PageMaker to open all other chapter files and modify their page numbers.

TIP

Although the individual files are still separate, there are features (such as printing, table of contents generation, and indexing) which can operate over the entire book.

Table of Contents (TOC)

Paragraph specifications   **OK**

Indents: Paragraph space: **Cancel**

Left `0` mm   Before `0` mm

First `0` mm   After `0` mm   **Rules...**

Right `0` mm   **Spacing...**

Alignment: `Left`   Dictionary: `UK English`

Options:

☐ Keep lines together   ☐ Keep with next `0` lines

☐ Column break before   ☐ Widow control `0` lines

☐ Page break before   ☐ Orphan control `0` lines

☒ Include in table of contents

At the bottom left corner of the Paragraph dialog box (Type menu), there is an option **Include in table of contents**.

Normally this option is set as part of the definition of heading or subheading styles of text (see chapter 11 "Style Sheets").

Creating a Table of Contents

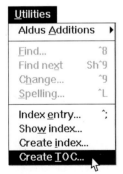

1.   Set the **Include in TOC** attribute (Paragraph dialog box) within your heading styles, and also to individual paragraphs if necessary.

2.   Choose **Create TOC** from the Utilities menu.

Create table of contents   **OK**

Title: `Contents`   **Cancel**

☐ Replace existing table of contents

☒ Include book publications

Format: ○ No page number

        ○ Page number before entry

        ● Page number after entry

Between entry and page number: `^t`

From this dialog box you can specify the TOC Title, as well as the format for the page references.
Note that a TOC can be compiled for a complete book list.

When PageMaker is ready, it will display a text-place symbol, allowing you to place the TOC on a suitable page:

Contents

Introduction	14
Primary Logos	14
THE HYBRID IMAGE	14
The House	15
THE TAPELOOP LOGO	16
THE FISH GRAPHIC	17
THE HYBRID IMAGE - PART TWO	18
Sectioning On	19
Tasteless Graphics	20
The key	20
The Second Incarnation	20
Other Concepts	21
The Need To Create	22
Appendix	22
Spleen	23
Pancreas	23
Rupture	23

Styles

Main Text
Running header
Section
Sub-Section
Subhead 1
Subhead 2
TOC Section
TOC Sub-Sectio
TOC Subhead 1
TOC title

If you look in the Style palette, you will see that new styles are created for each type of TOC entry. For example, the word Contents at the top of the table uses the style TOC title.

In the example above, three PageMaker styles had the Include in TOC attribute set. PageMaker located all instances of these and included them in the Contents page. It also created three new styles corresponding to these, plus TOC title.

You are obviously free to edit and format this new table in any way you wish, but if you make the changes by editing these new styles, then it will be easy to rebuild the TOC.

You will need to rebuild the TOC should you add any new entries, edit the main document text, or change the page numbering.

Rebuilding the TOC

By altering the TOC styles we can radically reformat the Contents page:

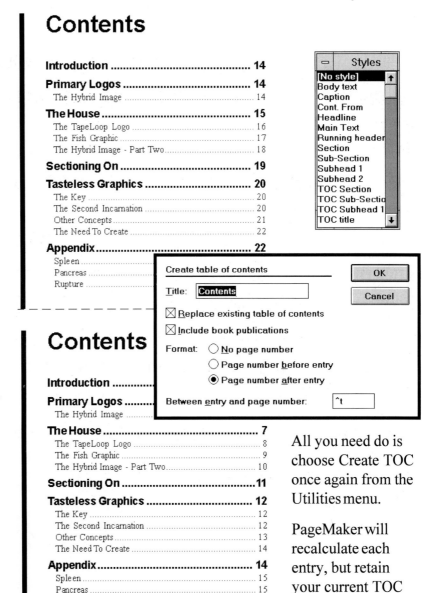

Contents

Introduction **14**
Primary Logos **14**
  The Hybrid Image 14
The House **15**
  The TapeLoop Logo 16
  The Fish Graphic 17
  The Hybrid Image - Part Two............................. 18
Sectioning On **19**
Tasteless Graphics **20**
  The Key 20
  The Second Incarnation 20
  Other Concepts 21
  The Need To Create 22
Appendix.. **22**
  Spleen ....
  Pancreas ....
  Rupture ....

Styles

[No style]
Body text
Caption
Cont. From
Headline
Main Text
Running header
Section
Sub-Section
Subhead 1
Subhead 2
TOC Section
TOC Sub-Sectio
TOC Subhead 1
TOC title

In this example, we renumbered the pages in our document, so needed to recreate the TOC...

Create table of contents

OK

Cancel

Title: Contents

☒ Replace existing table of contents
☒ Include book publications

Format: ○ No page number
       ○ Page number before entry
       ⦿ Page number after entry

Between entry and page number: ^t

Contents

Introduction ....
Primary Logos ....
  The Hybrid Image ....
The House **7**
  The TapeLoop Logo 8
  The Fish Graphic 9
  The Hybrid Image - Part Two............................. 10
Sectioning On **11**
Tasteless Graphics **12**
  The Key 12
  The Second Incarnation 12
  Other Concepts 13
  The Need To Create 14
Appendix.. **14**
  Spleen 15
  Pancreas 15
  Rupture 15

All you need do is choose Create TOC once again from the Utilities menu.

PageMaker will recalculate each entry, but retain your current TOC style definitions.

Indexing

Making An Index Entry

1. Select the relevant word or phrase with the Text tool.

2. Choose **Index entry** from the Utilities menu.

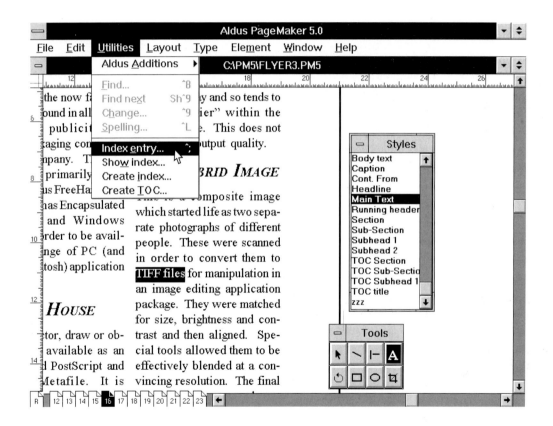

This operation can be carried out equally well from Layout or Story view.

TIP

The Index entry keyboard shortcut is Control and ; (semicolon).

The Index Entry Dialog Box

Add index entry

Type: ● <u>P</u>age reference ○ <u>C</u>ross-reference

Topic: Sort:

`TIFF files`

OK

Cancel

<u>A</u>dd

<u>T</u>opic...

Page range: ● <u>C</u>urrent page

○ To <u>n</u>ext style change

○ To next use <u>o</u>f style: `Body text` ±

○ <u>F</u>or next `1` paragraphs

○ <u>S</u>uppress page range

Page # override: ☐ <u>B</u>old ☐ <u>I</u>talic ☐ <u>U</u>nderline

TIP

To see how these entries finally appear, look over the example index at the end of this section.

3. For a simple index entry accepting the default settings, simply click **OK**. PageMaker will set up an index entry which keeps track of the selected text.

More Complex Entries

Use the Sort box to override the sort preferences:

In this example, the "Windows Metafile" entry will appear in the index under M rather than W.

Add index entry

Type: ● <u>P</u>age reference ○ <u>C</u>ross-reference

Topic: Sort:

`Windows Metafile` `Metafile`

OK

Cancel

<u>A</u>dd

<u>T</u>opic...

Page range: ● <u>C</u>urrent page

○ To <u>n</u>ext style change

○ To next use <u>o</u>f style: `Body text` ±

○ <u>F</u>or next `1` paragraphs

○ <u>S</u>uppress page range

Page # override: ☐ <u>B</u>old ☐ <u>I</u>talic ☐ <u>U</u>nderline

"Metafile" entered manually

Subtopics

You can make an entry part of a more major index topic, or subdivide it into subtopics (to a maximum of three levels):

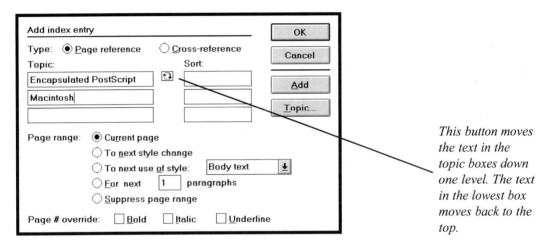

This button moves the text in the topic boxes down one level. The text in the lowest box moves back to the top.

Creating a Cross-Reference

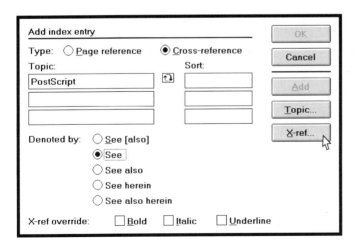

1. Click on the **Cross-reference** button at the top of the dialog box.

2. Choose the appropriate **Denoted by option**.

3. Click on the **X ref** button.

The following dialog box will appear:

Select the initial letter of the required topic using the Topic section pop-up menu, or click on the Next section button. A list of the existing entries will be displayed.

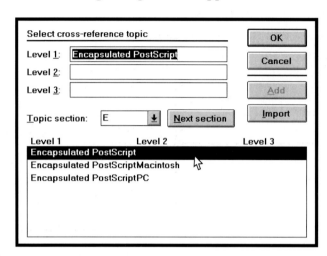

4. Locate and select the topic to which you wish to cross-reference.

Specifying a Range of Pages

Sometimes it is desirable to include a range of pages, rather than a single page reference next to an entry:

Here PageMaker will track a range of pages starting at the index entry, and ending at the next occurrence of text in the style "Section".

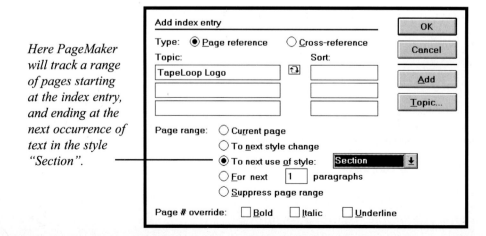

Creating the Index

1. Choose **Create index** from the Utilities menu.

2. Edit the Index title if necessary. Click on **Format** to customise the index appearance.

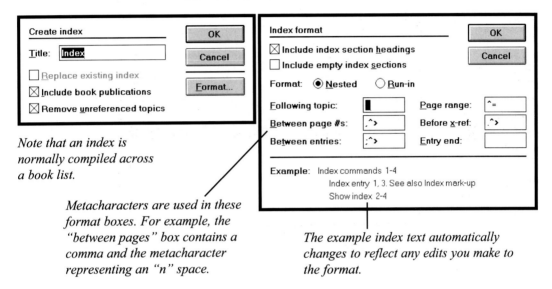

Note that an index is normally compiled across a book list.

Metacharacters are used in these format boxes. For example, the "between pages" box contains a comma and the metacharacter representing an "n" space.

The example index text automatically changes to reflect any edits you make to the format.

3. Click **OK**. PageMaker will look through all book publications for index entries. When it is ready, you will be presented with a loaded text icon.

4. Find a suitable place for the index and click. The new index story will flow onto the page.

The Example Index

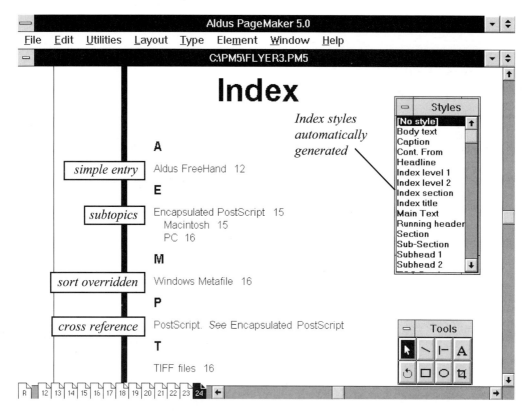

Index styles automatically generated

simple entry

subtopics

sort overridden

cross reference

The Story Editor

HINT

You can edit your index using Show index (Utility menu).

Rebuilding is the same as for Tables of Contents.

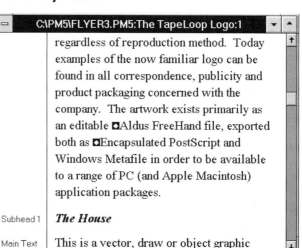

In the Story editor, index markers show up as inverse diamond shapes. You can search and replace using the index marker metacharacter (^;).

CHAPTER

17

Printing

This chapter covers...

**The Print Document
Dialog Box**

**The Print Options
Dialog Box**

**The Print Colours
Dialog Box**

**The Print Setup
Dialog Box**

Printer Styles

The Print Document Dialog Box

1. Choose **Print** from the File menu. The following dialog box will appear:

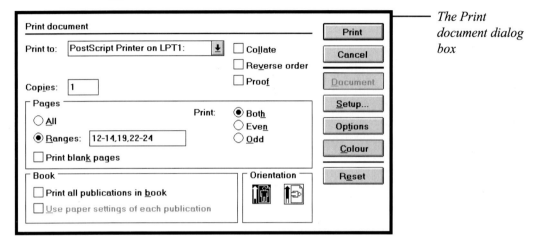

The Print document dialog box

2. Your target printer should already be specified, if not select from the **Print to** pop-up menu.

3. Choose the number of copies.

4. Select the pages to print. Note that you can specify a set of discontinuous pages: in the example above we are asking to print pages 12 to 14 (inclusive), page 19, and pages 22 to 24.

5. Note the other options (print entire book, collate, reverse order).

6. You can now either click directly on the **Print** button, or view the other Print dialog boxes by clicking on **Setup**, **Options** or **Colour**.

The Print Options Dialog Box

NOTE

The options available will depend on the capabilities of your printer.

Tiling is used when printing a document larger than the page size of the printer.

In this case each page is printed as a series of "tiles" which are manually reassembled.

The Print Colours Dialog Box

NOTE

If you choose Composite on a monochrome printer, the colours will be converted to halftone greyscales.

Forcing all colours to black will usually speed up printing.

You can choose to print a colour composite (for colour printers), or separations.

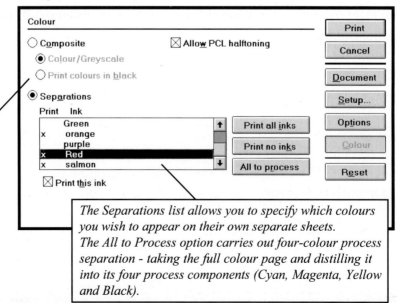

The Separations list allows you to specify which colours you wish to appear on their own separate sheets.
The All to Process option carries out four-colour process separation - taking the full colour page and distilling it into its four process components (Cyan, Magenta, Yellow and Black).

The Print Setup Dialog Box

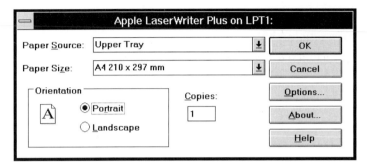

This is the standard Windows Print Setup dialog.

The settings and options will depend on the current printer driver selected.

Printer Styles

You have seen that there is a vast multitude of print options (four dialog boxes in total). To cut out the tedious process of making the same settings time and again as you switch printers, there is an Aldus Addition which lets you define and access Printer Styles:

1. Choose **Printer styles** from the Additions submenu.

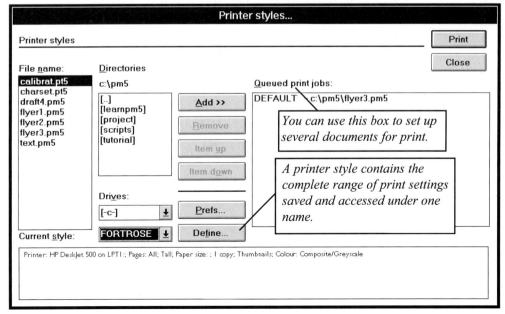

You can use this box to set up several documents for print.

A printer style contains the complete range of print settings saved and accessed under one name.

2.   Click on **Define** to set up your own Print styles. The following dialog box will appear:

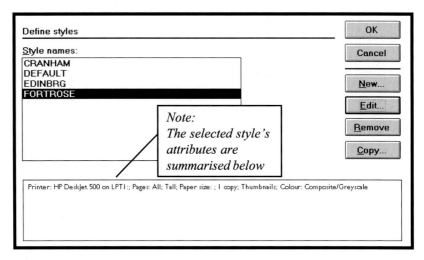

3.   Select a style to change, or click on **New**. Enter a name for a new style.

You will be taken to the **Print document** dialog box.

4.   Make the necessary settings. You can also click on **Options**, **Colour** or **Setup** in the same way as when printing normally from the File menu.

5.   Click **OK** when finished. The new style will be available from the Printer styles menu option in future.

This feature is invaluable if you consistently work with several different printers or documents which require specific types of print options.

CHAPTER

18

Tips and Techniques

This chapter covers...

Interruptible Screen Redraw

Panose Font Matching

The Magnify Tool

Accessing Documents created in an earlier version of PageMaker

The Library Palette

Cross Platform Compatibility

Template Documents

Compressing TIFF files

Creating your own Templates

The Time Stamp Import Filter

Copying from One Document to Another

Special Keyboard Characters

Using an Outside Printing Service

Keyboard Shortcut Summary

Tips for Good Document Design

Interruptible Screen Redraw

It often takes your machine a long time to update the screen display, particularly if there is a high level of detail and colour.

It is not necessary to wait for a complete redraw all the time. If you go ahead and access a menu option, PageMaker will stop redrawing and respond immediately.

The Magnify Tool

This offers another way to zoom in and out.

To Zoom In

1.   Hold down **Control** and **Space**. You pointer will turn into a positive magnify tool.

2.   Point to the area where you want to zoom in and click.

3.   Alternatively use the tool to draw a rectangle area (drag with the mouse). When you release the mouse button PageMaker will zoom in to fill the screen with this area.

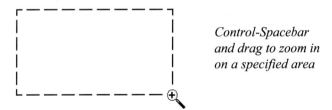

Control-Spacebar and drag to zoom in on a specified area

4.   To access the negative magnify tool, hold down the **Alt** key as well as the others. This allows you to zoom back out again.

The Library Palette

This palette can be used to store commonly required PageMaker elements.

1.   Make sure that the **Library palette** option is active (Window menu). The current library will appear.

2.   To add an element to the library, simply select it and then click on the + symbol. A thumbnail image of the object will appear in the palette.

3.   Whenever you require another copy of the element, simply drag it out of the palette back into the document.

The Options Menu

If you click on **Options** in the palette, a menu will appear. This allows you to create your own custom libraries, or open existing libraries.

Item Information

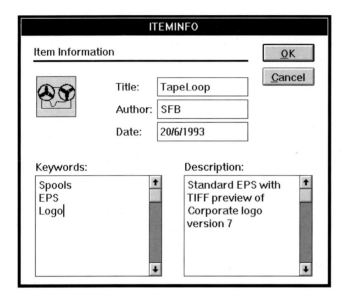

If you double click on a library item, this dialog box will appear.

This gives you the opportunity to enter reference information for the element.

NOTE

The options menu is normally set to automatically display this dialog box whenever a new element is added.

The Search Dialog Box

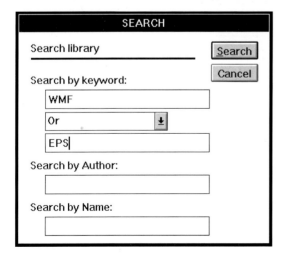

If you choose **Search** from the Options menu this dialog box will appear.

It allows you to search for specific library items. You can enter search-text based on the contents of the keyword, author, or name field. When you click **Search** the palette will only display elements which match the search criteria.

Template Documents

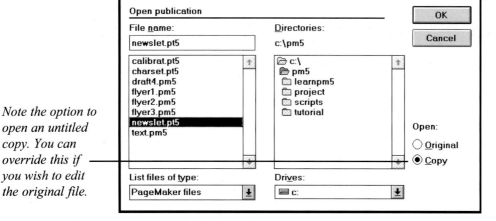

Note the option to open an untitled copy. You can override this if you wish to edit the original file.

A template document has a PT5, rather than a PM5 extension. PageMaker will tend to open a copy (rather than the original) when **Open** is chosen from the File menu.

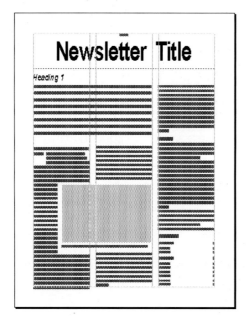

A template is actually a normal PageMaker document. It has normally been designed as a blueprint, a specimen for you to adapt to your own needs.

This template is a newsletter created using dummy text and FPO (for position only) graphic boxes.

Using a Template

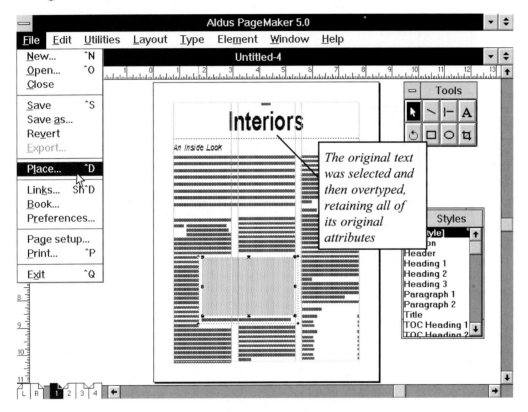

Retyping Text

Retype any small pieces of dummy text by selecting first with the Text tool. The original text attributes will remain as you overtype.

Replacing Graphic Elements

1. Select a dummy graphic with the pointer tool. Choose **Place** from the File menu.

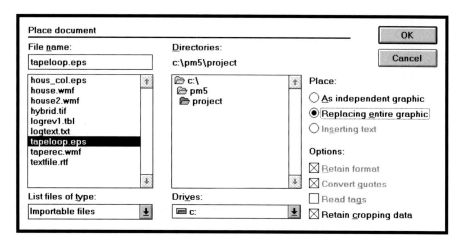

2. From the Place dialog box, make sure that the **Replacing entire graphic** option is active. If it is greyed out then there is no element currently selected - click Cancel and repeat step 1.

The imported element will replace the original, retaining its position, size and text wrap properties.

NOTE

Single or threaded text blocks can also be replaced using this method.

Creating your own Templates

If you need to produce a consistent series of documents (e.g. reports where the contents vary from month to month but the design remains the same), then it is a good idea to create a template:

1.   Create the PageMaker document in the normal way. It is usual to use dummy text and grey boxes for graphics to be replaced.

2.   Choose **Save** from the File menu.

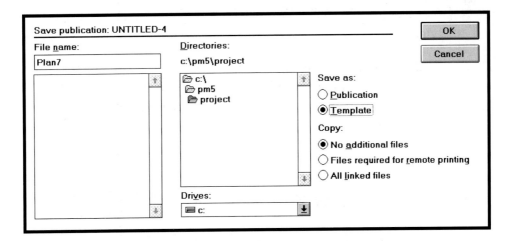

3.   Click on the option to Save as a Template. Click **OK**.

A PT5 document will be created. Another advantage of using templates is that they can be used by someone with minimal design/typography experience, since that part of the document-generation process has already been completed by the template designer.

Copying from One Document to Another

1. Open both documents in turn (File menu).

2. Choose **Tile** from the Window menu:

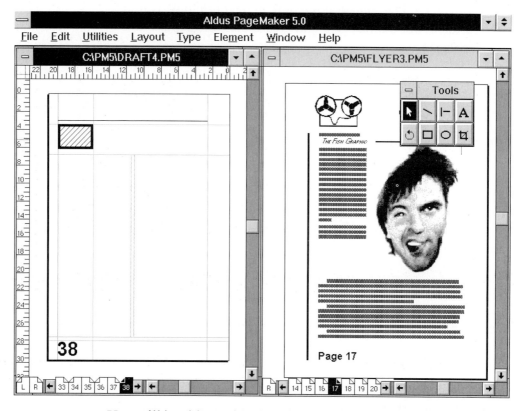

You will be able to view both publications side by side.

3. Locate the item to be copied in one document, then move to the proposed destination in the second.

4. Simply drag the element from one document to the other (the original will not be removed from the first document).

graphic dragged from one document to the other

NOTE

As you drag the element from the first document, on nearing the layout window border PageMaker will tend to start scrolling horizontally. Ignore this and carry on dragging into the next window.

Using an Outside Printing Service

If you are sending a document somewhere else for printing, it is important that all the necessary ingredients are included. This includes imported files for which there are no copies within the publication (check **Link options** to review this), and fonts used (check using the **Pub Info** Addition).

In the Save as dialog box there is an option which instructs PageMaker to automatically copy all files required for remote printing:

Copy:
- ⦿ No additional files
- ○ Files required for remote printing
- ○ All linked files

NOTE

It is very important that your target printer matches the type used by the bureau (i.e. the final output device), no matter which printer you use for proofing. This affects the fonts available and text spacing information. If you change printer type be prepared for elements to move as the publication is recomposed.

Printing a PostScript File to Disk

If the printing bureau does not have the same version of PageMaker or the fonts that you use, then there will be problems involved in sending them a copy of your document.

One way around this is to generate a "printed" PostScript file from your own machine. This can include all necessary font information as well as graphic files needed at print time. The printing bureau does not even require PageMaker itself.

1.   Choose **Print** from the File menu.

2.   Click the **Setup** button.

3.   Make sure that a PostScript printer is selected. Click **Options**.

▷

The following dialog box appears:

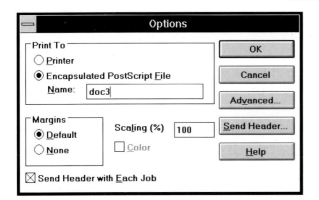

The options available within this dialog box will depend on the printer and printer driver currently selected.

4.   Under **Print to,** click on **Encapsulated PostScript File**. Enter a suitable filename. Click **OK**.

5.   When you click on **Print**, the PostScript file will be generated.

TIP

Remember that you can define these settings as part of a Printer style, as explained earlier.

NOTE

You may need to ask the outside printing service for a copy of the PPD and PDX file which relates to their imagesetting device.

PPD (PostScript Printer Description) and PDX (Printer Description eXtension) files contain details about the Printer (such as fonts available) which allows PageMaker to decide on exactly what needs to go into the Encapsulated PostScript file.

Panose Font Matching

Sometimes you open a document which made use of fonts not available in your current system. In this case the following dialog appears...

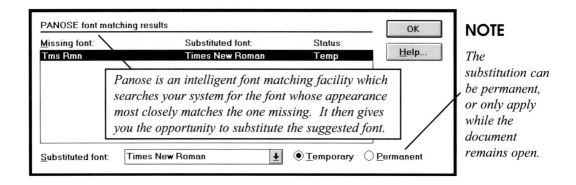

NOTE

The substitution can be permanent, or only apply while the document remains open.

Panose Options

1. Choose **Preferences** from the File menu.

2. Click on **Map fonts**. The following dialog box will appear:

If a suitable match cannot be found, PageMaker will resort to the default font specified here

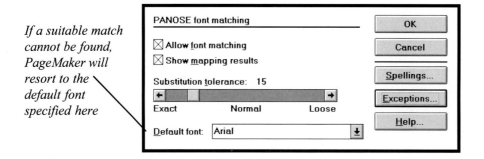

Here you can activate/deactivate automatic font matching, and set the substitution tolerance. A loose tolerance allows substitution even if the closest font is a poor match. Selecting "Exact" will cause PageMaker only to substitute if it finds an exact match.

Other options within this dialog box:

Show mapping results

If you switch off this option, then PageMaker will carry out modifications without displaying the Font matching results dialog box.

Spellings

Often a single font has different spellings for the Windows and Macintosh platform. This option allows you to specify each spelling. PageMaker is then able to identify these as the same font.

Exceptions

This options lets you set up customised substitutions. You can specify which available fonts will replace which missing fonts. You can replace a number of fonts with a single substitute. All settings are saved in a substitutions file, and so act as global preferences.

Accessing Documents created in an earlier version of PageMaker

1. Choose **Open** from the File menu.

2. Under **List files of type**, choose **Older PageMaker documents**.

3. Select the file and click **OK**.

The file will be converted to a new untitled PageMaker 5 document.

Cross Platform Compatibility

Opening a Macintosh Document in Windows

1. Use a suitable transfer utility to make the Macintosh file available to Windows (e.g. Apple File Exchange, Access PC or a multi-platform network).

2. Choose **Open** from the File menu.

3. Under **List files of type**, choose **All files.**

4. Select the file and click **OK**. The file will be translated according to two sets of decisions:

1. Font Matching

The fonts available on each platform are likely to differ. See the section on Panose font matching earlier in this chapter.

2. Translation between PICT and WMF

The platform standards for graphic objects are PICT (Macintosh) and Windows Metafile (Windows).

PageMaker will give you the option to convert placed graphics from one format to the other, so that the printable image and screen representation are available under the new platform.

Sometimes the Links option has been set so that there is no copy of a placed file within the Publication (see chapter 15 "Links"), instead PageMaker makes use of a link to the original graphic file. In this case it is best to re-import the files from the new platform (PageMaker can import both PICT and WMF files, converting them to the current platform if necessary).

NOTE

This issue may also affect Macintosh EPS files, which often use a PICT screen preview image. In this case conversion allows the graphic to be viewed on screen. It does not affect printing quality which will always be to the high standard of EPS.

TIP

If you intend to return the publication to the original platform after editing, do not convert the files. The reason for this is that conversion may carry with it a degradation of quality due to the intrinsically different nature of the two file formats.

Compressing TIFF files

TIFF files can take up a lot of space on disk and within a document, depending on their size, resolution and number of colours/grey levels.

PageMaker has built-in LZW (Lempel-Ziv & Welch) TIFF compression, which works by making a compressed copy of the file without changing the original.

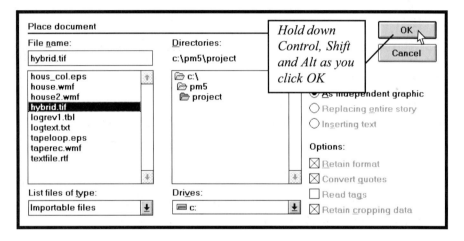

1.   Choose **Place** from the File menu.

2.   For moderate compression:

     Select the file then hold down **Control** and **Alt** as you click **OK**. Keep these keys held down for a few seconds afterwards.

     For maximum compression:

     As above, but hold down **Control**, **Shift** and **Alt**.

The compression efficiency will depend on the contents of the graphic. In this example the original was compressed to less than a fifth of its original size.

Name	Size (bytes)
hybrid.tif	185520
hybrid_d.tif	37412
hybrid_m.tif	35322

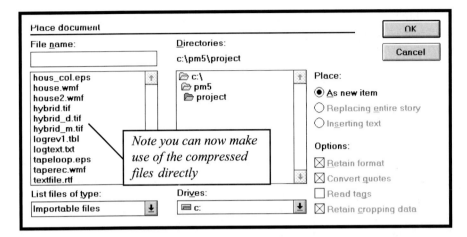

Note you can now make use of the compressed files directly

PageMaker will compress the TIFF file, saving the new version in the same directory. To avoid a name clash, the following characters are appended according to compression type:

Monochrome or Palette Colour Images:

"_P" is added to a moderately compressed file, "_L" to one with maximum compression.

Greyscale or Full Colour Images:

"_D" is added to a moderately compressed file, "_M" to one with maximum compression.

Decompressing TIFF files

You may wish to do this if you have lost or deleted the original file, and would like to use the graphic in an application which does not support LZW compression:

1.   Choose **Place** from the File menu.

2.   Select the file and hold down **Control** as you click **OK**.

The decompressed file will have the characters "_U" added to the original filename.

The Time Stamp Import Filter

This allows PageMaker to print the current time/date by reading the system clock:

1.   Choose **Place** from the File menu.

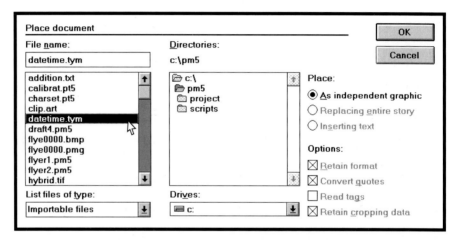

2.   Select the file "datetime.tym". Click **OK**.

3.   Choose the required format option from the pop-up menu.

4.   Select a suitable font. Click **OK**.

The current date appears, surprisingly, as a graphic.

4/7/93

You can now place the date/time stamp as a normal draw-type graphic. Note that this allows you to resize by dragging directly on a handle.

^ represents Control key

Special Keyboard Characters

Description		**Keyboard Command**
Bullet	•	^ Shift 8
Copyright symbol	©	^ Shift O (letter "O", not zero)
Paragraph marker	¶	^ Shift 7
Open quote	'	^ [
Close quote	'	^]
Open double quote	"	^ Shift [
Close double quote	"	^ Shift]
Registered trademark	®	^ Shift G
Section marker	§	^ Shift 6
En space		^ Shift N
Em space		^ Shift M
Thin space		^ Shift T
Non-breaking (hard) space	^	Shift H
Discretionary soft hyphen		^ ~
Non-breaking hyphen	-	^ Shift ~
Non-breaking slash	/	^ Shift /
En dash	–	^ =
Em dash	—	^ Shift =
Page no. marker		^ Shift 3
New line (soft return)		Shift Enter

^ represents Control key

Keyboard Shortcut Summary

File menu

New	^N
Open	^O
Save	^S
Place	^D
Links	^ Shift D
Print	^P
Exit	^Q
Save all publications	Shift "Save"
Close all publications	Shift "Close"
Revert to last mini-save	Shift "Revert"
Copy book list to all publications	^ "Book"

Edit menu

Undo	^Z or Alt Backspace
Cut	^X or Shift Delete
Copy	^C or ^ Insert
Paste	^V or Shift Insert
Clear	Delete
Select all	^A
Story/Layout view	^E
Power paste	^ Shift P
Multiple paste bypassing dialog box	Shift "Multiple paste"
Close current story only	^ Shift E (from Story view)
Close all stories in current publication	Shift "Close story"

Utilities

Find	^8
Find next	Shift ^9
Spelling	^L
Index entry	^;

Show index for current publication only

^ "Show index"

Make index entry bypassing dialog box	^ Shift ;
Add proper name to index	^ Shift Z

Layout menu

Fit in window	^W
25% view	^0 (zero)
50% view	^5
75% view	^7
Actual size	^1
200% view	^2
400% view	^4
Show pasteboard	^ Shift W
Actual size/Fit in window toggle	Right button
Actual size/200% toggle	Shift Right button
Set view for all pages	^ Alt Page view
Set page to Fit in Window	Shift Click on page icon
Rulers	^R
Snap to rulers	^ Shift Y
Guides	^J
Snap to guides	^U
Goto page	^G
Cycle through pages until mouse click	Shift "Goto page"

Type menu

Type specs	^T
Paragraph	^M
Indents/tabs	^I
Hyphenation	^H
Define styles	^3
Increase font size 1 point	^ Shift >

Decrease font size 1 point	^ Shift <
Increase font to next standard size	^ >
Decrease font to next standard size	^ <
Left align	^ Shift L
Right align	^ Shift R
Centre	^ Shift C
Justify	^ Shift J
Force Justify	^ Shift F
All caps on/off	^ Shift K
Subscript	^\
Superscript	^ Shift \
Autoleading	^ Shift A
Normal width	^ Shift X
No tracking	^ Shift Q
Bold	^ Shift B
Italic	^ Shift I
Underline	^ Shift U
Strikethrough	^ Shift S
Normal	^ Shift Space
Reverse	^ Shift V

Element menu

Bring to front	^F
Send to back	^B

Window menu

Toolbox	^6
Style palette	^Y
Colour palette	^K
Control palette	^ ' (single quote)
Cascade all open stories	Shift "Cascade"
Tile all open stories	Shift "Tile"

^ represents Control key

Help menu

Contents	F1
Help within dialog box	
	Shift Right button
Context sensitive help	
	Shift F1
List installation options	
	^ "About PageMaker"

Toolbox

Line tool	Shift F2
Perpendicular line	Shift F3
Text tool	Shift F4
Rotation tool	Shift F5
Rectangle tool	Shift F6
Ellipse tool	Shift F7
Cropping tool	Shift F8
Zoom in	^ Spacebar
Zoom out	^ Alt Spacebar
Toggle between current tool and pointer	F9

Control palette

Focus on control palette	^ `
Character/paragraph mode toggle	^ Shift ~
Next option	Tab
Previous option	Shift Tab
Select reference point	Numeric keypad
Revert to last valid value	Esc
Apply	Enter
Apply retaining focus on Control palette	Shift Enter
Activate/deactivate current button	Spacebar
Change unit of measure	Shift F11
Nudge	Arrow keys
Nudge by 10 times the normal amount	^ Arrow keys

Select tracking, style or font name
Type first few characters

Style palette

Edit	^ Click on name
New	^ Click on "no style"

Colour palette

Edit	^ Click on name
New	
	^ Click on "Registration"
Toggle between spot and process colour	
	^ Alt Shift Click on name

Graphics

Draw regular shape	Shift
Select multiple objects	
	Shift Click
Select object behind	^ Click
Horizontal or vertical move	
	Shift drag
Restore proportions	
	Shift Click on corner handle
Proportional stretch	
	Shift stretch
Resize bitmap to printer resolution	^ stretch

Text

Select word	Double click
Select paragraph	Triple click
Move up/down screen	Pg Up/Pg Dn
Move to beginning/end of line	Home/End
Move to beginning/end of sentence	^ Home/^ End
Move to beginning/end of story	^ Pg Up/^ Pg Dn

Move left/right one word
^ left/right arrow
Move up/down one paragraph
^ up/down arrow

Kern 0.01 em space	
	^ Shift Keypad + or -
Kern 0.04 em space	
	^ Keypad + or -
Remove manual kerning	
	^ Shift 0 (zero)

Print dialog box

Set options without printing
Shift Click on "Print"

Place dialog box

Moderate TIFF compression	
	^ Alt "OK"
(Wait a few seconds before releasing these keys)	
Maximum TIFF compression	
	^ Alt Shift "OK"
Decompress TIFF	^ "OK"

General

Exit from nested dialog boxes	
	Shift "OK" or "Cancel"
Auto/Manual text flow	^
Semi-auto text flow	Shift
Edit OLE object	Double click
Edit non-OLE object	
	Alt Double click
Choose Editor for object	
	Shift Alt Double click
Switch to next open Publication	^F6
Redraw page at high resolution	^ Shift Page view
Previous/Next page	F11/F12
Grabber hand	Alt Drag

Tips for Good Document Design

- Use the Master pages as fully as possible to set up a consistent design which is carried throughout your document.

- Use columns and guidelines to create a layout grid. If you keep text and graphic elements aligned to this grid then your document will assume a clear structure.

- Try not to use too many fonts or text effects. Often good results can be gained from restricting yourself to two basic fonts, one for headings and one for body text.

- Allow yourself the use of white space. It is usually not necessary to completely fill each page.

- Make sure that text is always readable. Too many characters to a line, or too little space between lines (leading) can create a solid mass of text which is very tiring to read.

- Use style sheets as much as possible. This way you have the flexibility to make design alterations to, for example, all of your headings in one simple manoeuvre at any time.

- Feel free to experiment with dummy text and graphics on the page in the early stages of your design. Try to form a clear idea of your document margins, text columns and page structure right from the beginning.

- Keep your design as simple and consistent as possible.

Index

A

Actual size   17
Aldus Additions   145
  Balance columns   147
  Build booklet   148
  Continuation line   147
  Create colour library   150
  Create keyline   151
  Drop capitals   152
  Edit tracks   153
  Expert kerning   155
  Find overset text   157
  Open stories   157
  Open template   155
  Printer styles   157
  PS Group-it   156
  PS Ungroup-it   156
  Publication info   151
  Run script   157
  Sort pages   146
  Story info   152
  Textblock info   152
  Traverse textblocks   146
Aldus Setup   62
Alignment   42. *See also*
  Guidelines
Apply button   37
Attributes button   125
Autoflow   96

B

Baseline shift   81
Bitmapped graphics   63
Bold   73
Book   181
Boxes   32

C

Change   125
Characters

Special   217
Clipboard   47
Closing   28
Colour
  Palette   14, 139
Colour separation. *See*
    Printing: Colours
Colours
  Creating new colours   139
  Editing   141
  Importing   142
  Libraries   142
  Process   141
  Spot   139
Column breaks   110
Column guides   100
Compose to printer   22
Compressing TIFF files   214
Contrast   68
Control   67
Control
  palette   14, 37, 39, 85
  Repositioning mode   39
  Resizing mode   41
Copy   47
Copy master guides   99
Cropping   66
  Using Control palette   86
Cross platform
  compatibility   212
Cross referencing. *See*
    Indexing: Cross-references
Custom line   45
Cut   47

D

Date/Time Import   216
Decompressing TIFF
  files   215
Defaults
  Graphics   54
  Restoring   56

Text   75
Define styles   131
Deleting elements   33
Desktop Publishing   11
Dictionaries   106, 124
  Adding to   116
Document
  Window   13
Document design   220
Double-sided document   22
Draw graphics   65

E

Earlier PageMaker
    versions   212
Edit colour   142
Edit menu   35, 47, 49
Edit story   123
Element menu   44, 68, 85
Ellipses   32
Encapsulated
    PostScript   65, 209
Microsoft Excel   178

F

Facing pages   22
File Manager   12
File menu   21, 61, 91
Fill   45
Fill and line   44
Find   125
Fit in window   17
Floating palettes   14
Fonts   151
Force justification   74
Aldus FreeHand   65, 142

G

Global defaults   55
Goto page   25

Graphic file formats   63
Grouping elements. *See* Aldus
    Additions: PS Group-It
Guidelines   51
    Column   100
    Horizontal   52
    Locking   53
    Using   53
    Vertical   51

H

Handles   34
Hyphenation   106, 116

I

Image control   68
Import filters   62
Importing
    Text. *See* Place: Text
Imposition. *See* Aldus
    Additions: Build booklet
Include in TOC   182
Indents/Tabs   74, 113
Indexing   185
    Create index   189
    Cross-references   187
    Index examples   190
    Making an entry   185
    Page range   188
    Subtopics   187
    Types of entry   186
Inline graphics   117
Inserting pages   26
Interruptible screen
    redraw   199
Introduction   11
Inverted image   68
Invisible characters   128
Irregular columns   101

J

Justification   74

K

Keep with   109
Kerning 78. *See also* Aldus
    Additions: Expert kerning
Keyboard characters   217
Keyboard shortcuts   18, 218

L

Layout menu   18, 25, 53, 99
Layout view   127
Leaders   114
Leading   73
Library palette   200
    Options   200
    Search   201
Lightness   68
Line   31, 44
    Custom   45
Links   151, 175
    Hot links   176
    Link Info   175
    Link options   176
    Link status   177
    Unlink   177
    Using Windows   178
Loaded graphic icon   61
LZW compression   214

M

Macintosh platform   212
Magnetic guidelines. *See*
    Guidelines
Magnify tool   199
Margins   22
Master pages   25, 99
Metacharacters   126
Mini-save   25
Moving elements   34
Multiple paste   49

N

New   13, 21

New publication   21
Number of pages   21
Numbers   23
Numeric control   37

O

Opening a document   12
Opening a publication   24
Orphans   107
Outside printing   208
Ovals   32

P

Page   13
    Dimensions   21
    Orientation   21
Page breaks   110
Page icons   25, 99
Page numbering   181
Page setup   21, 55
Page views   17, 18
PageMaker
    EXE file   12
    Icon   12
    Screen   13
    Window   13
Paint files   63
Panose font
    matching   210, 212
    Exceptions   211
    Map fonts   210
    Spellings   211
Pantone   142
Paper fill   46
Paragraph rules   111
Paragraph specifications   106
Paste   47
Pasteboard   13
Perpendicular lines   31
Aldus PhotoStyler   63
PICT   213
Place   61, 117
    Text   91
PM5.CNF file   56

Power pasting   48
Preferences   15, 123
Printing
  Colours   194
  Document   193
  Options   194
  PostScript to disk   208
  Printer styles   195
  Setup   195
Program Manager   12

R

Rectangles   32
Red triangle   92
Reference point   39
Reflecting   85, 87
Remove transformation   85
Removing pages   26
Resizing elements   34
Resolution   63
  Matching   67
Restart page numbering   22
Rotation   57
  Angle   57
  Using Control palette   88
Rulers   15

S

Saving   27
Screening   68
Select all   35
Selecting elements   33
Selecting multiple
    elements   35
Selection box   36
Set width   81
Shift   31, 35, 64
Shift-click   35
Show pasteboard   18
Skewing   85, 87
Small Caps   105
Snap to   51
Spell checking   106, 124
Start page #   21

Starting up   12
Story editor   123
  Styles   135
Story view   127
Style. *See* Text: Paragraph
    styles
Style palette   14
Subscript   105
Superscript   105

T

Table Editor
  Text
    Importing   163
Table editor   161
  Borders   168
  Exporting   170
  Fills   169
  Grouping cells   165
  Lines   167
  Links with PageMaker   172
  Number format   169
  Saving   170
  Table dimensions   164
  Tables in PageMaker   171
  Text
    Changing attributes   166
    Entering   162
Table of Contents   182
  Creating   182
  Rebuilding   184
Tabulation   113
Templates   202
  Creating   205
  Replacing elements   203
  Using   203
Text
  Adding   71
  Alignment   74
  Attributes
    Character level   73
    Paragraph level   74
  Blocks   76
  Control palette   72
  Editing   72

Paragraph styles   131
Reverse   73
Ruler   113
Selecting   72
Style by example   134
Threaded   92
Tool   71
Text wrap
  Irregular   120
  Regular   119
TIFF
  Compressing   214
  File format   63
  Preview image   65
Toolbox   14
Tracking 79. *See also* Aldus
    Additions: Edit tracks
Triple click   72
Type menu   106
Type specifications   105

U

Utilities menu   125

W

Widows   107
Window menu   14, 24
Windows metafile   65, 213
Windowshade handles   76

Z

Zero Point
  Repositioning   16
Zooming in and out   199

Training and Consultancy

Companies and individuals seeking training or consultancy on any computer software package (Introductory to Advanced level) should write to or call Computer Step at the location below.

Quantity Discounts

For quantity discounts on this book or any of our other books, contact:

Computer Step   Tel. 0926 817999
Unit 5c, Southfield Road   Fax. 0926 817005
Southam, Leamington Spa
Warwickshire
CV33 OJH